Breaking from Your Parents

Setting a New Precedent for Your Life and Our Species

Daniel Mackler
www.wildtruth.net
New York City, 2014

*I dedicate this book to all who wish
to break from the lies of their parents,
get real and start something new*

Table of Contents

A Few Words on This Book's Structure

This book is divided into three main sections. The first, which follows the introduction and a few personal words about me, provides background on the subject of breaking from parents from a wide-angle lens, both theoretical and practical. The second section addresses actions we can take during the process of breaking with our parents: actions to maximize the healthiness of our breaking up process and minimize the risk to ourselves. The third section looks forward: toward our new life. It explores not only things that others have discovered in their longer-range processes of breaking from their parents, but things that might someday come to be—with themselves as individuals and us all as a species.

Acknowledgments

I wish to acknowledge four people for helping bring this work to fruition: Phil Crimmins, Phil Johnston, Jake Desyllas and Hannah Braime. Each read a draft of this book and provided invaluable literary feedback—and additionally, Phil Johnston designed the book's cover. All four of you have my deepest gratitude—and my friendship. This work is stronger for your gifts and your hard-won life experience. Thank you.

Introduction

When I began my journey into breaking from my parents, I had no good resources and no true allies. I had a few fictional books for partial inspiration, such as *My Side of the Mountain* and *Siddhartha*, but I knew of no actual person who had done anything resembling what I was attempting and I had no one to encourage, much less guide, my path. Although I did see people who rebelled against their parents through the lenses of drugs, clothing, sex, religion and music I somehow couldn't connect with their rebellion, which too often struck me as unconscious, self-destructive and, below the radical surface trappings, essentially conventional. I also saw ways in which my own parents had rebelled against their parents, but their rebellion seemed flawed to me because their parents still exerted profound control over their lives.

It took me a while to get my journey going. I was pretty lost at first. Almost everything I knew about what I was supposed to do with my life came from the mandates of my family and society: love your parents, forgive their errors, accept their flaws, honor their wishes, bury your rage, deny the lies they've told you since the dawning of your memory, find a partner, have children and then teach them to do the same. I tried to live this way but was not very good at it. I was too real. And I was also too hurt. I had no choice but to move forward—to heal and find something better.

In the last twenty or so years I have taken great strides in breaking from my parents and, more fundamentally, breaking from their lies. This has been a rigorous and ongoing process and has not happened all at once. My path has taken many twists and turns and has been full of errors, successes and experiments. I have stayed away from them for years at a time yet several times have gone back to test the waters and even run back for respite, only to leave once again. There have been times in which I have not spoken with them for years and other times when I spoke with them fairly regularly. I am now 41 years old and haven't spoken with or seen them in four years and have no plans to do so.

I have also, for years, been fairly open about my process of breaking away, in order to optimize my learning. I have shared my experiences and my developing point of view with countless friends, relatives, therapists, parents, curious people, email correspondents and at times even my own parents themselves, and have collected a wealth of replies, disagreements, criticisms, personal stories and, more recently, even support. I was also a therapist myself for more than ten of the last twenty years, which offered me a most intimate window into others' lives, others' childhoods and others' relationships with their parents. All this information, combined with my own experience, creates the base of data for this book.

My goal in these pages is to provide you a voice of support on your shoulder and perhaps, if I have written it well, some new perspective. This, I hope, will augment the truth already within you. I have also tried to do here what I wished someone had done with me at certain points in my life when I was more embroiled in the process of breaking up with my parents: be direct! That said, I don't want to tell anyone what to do, because I didn't want anyone telling me what to do and still don't. But in my writing I do come to real conclusions based on my experiences and assessments, and I don't tiptoe around these conclusions for the sake of politeness or societal acceptance. I'd rather avoid wasting time and speak clearly. For that reason, I have not written this book for people who are committed to staying close to their parents. Had I written it for that audience I would have made the book ten times longer and provided endless defenses and proofs for points that are, to this book's proper audience, more self-evident. And I would have likely convinced this improper audience of little anyway, because people's emotionally-rooted reasons for staying with their parents tend to be impervious to intellectual logic.

Thus, this book does not try to prove that you were damaged by your parents; it assumes it. Why else, after all, would you consider breaking from them and trying something new? Nor does this book try to prove that your parents' messages were, at the least, partially laden with their own denial or lies; it assumes that too. Nor does this book try to defend your parents' feelings and perspective for the sake of "fairness" or "balance" or "compassion for them"; it sides squarely with you, that is, you who defend the child you once were and the hurt child that part of you still remains. Hasn't their point of view been prioritized enough?

But this book does provide arguments that many could find controversial. For instance, I believe that the world would be better off if we all took more steps to break from our parents. As someone who holds individual growth, emotional health, attainment of self-knowledge and usefulness to others to be the highest purposes in life, I see no other way. Staying close to our parents, even if our parents are relatively healthy compared to the norm, keeps us stuck in the family perspective, beholden to the hurts they inflicted upon us and bound to pass them on to others. Yet at the same time I respect that the decision to break away from one's parents — or not to — is entirely a personal one. Again, I see it as no one's business, mine included, to tell anyone what to do with his or her life — or when to do it. But if you do wish to break away, I support you fully. I think the world desperately needs more people who break away from their parents and try something new.

Yet this is more than just a book of support. This book is also an exploration. It explores people leaving the cult of the family system. It explores people breaking primally held taboos that stunt our growth. It explores people breaking family secrets and thus committing family-defined crimes. It explores the courage of people facing their deepest childhood terrors against seemingly overwhelming odds. It explores people facing rejection not only from the figures who created their existence but also their siblings, their extended families, their social networks, their friends, their teachers and their very societal mores. It explores family warfare, with battle lines drawn in the sand and people picking sides. And it explores the harsh consequences of this war: slander, spies, betrayal and emotional torture.

But this book also explores rebirth. It is an exploration of liberation. It is an exploration of people finding a new life, new friends, new family, new love, new perspective and newfound respect for the self—and hope. It is an exploration of sacrifice for a purpose, trust in something deeper and a connection with the indomitable self within. It is an exploration of the process of delving into the guts of our inner beauty and believing in this beauty more than we believe the lies branded into us when we were young and vulnerable. It is an exploration of our right to question some of our most firmly held beliefs and to continue to question under pressure of rejections that would have killed us when we were younger and more dependent. It is an exploration of our path toward growing stronger, standing up firmly and acknowledging our strength. It is an exploration of a new way of interacting, a new code of ethics and a new inspiration. And it is also an exploration of a newly awakening breed of truth-tellers, a new template for social revolution and a new society-to-be.

A Few Words About Me

My family deeply loved me in some ways and deeply wounded me in others. Although they provided me a certain base of nurturance and support and were, from what I have observed, much better than most parents in the world, I suffered painfully under the tyranny of their own unresolved childhood wounds. Although they always said that I could become whatever I wanted in my life, that didn't mean that I was allowed to be *whomever* I wanted. They could not tolerate me being a whole, integrated self and made it clear to me from an early age which parts of my psyche were not allowed to exist. They forced whole parts of me into hiding and forced many of my natural reactions of pain and anger and resentment into hiding as well.

My father was a gifted, respected lawyer in my hometown. He defended criminals of all stripes and he explained to me the value of a legal system of lawyers, judges, juries and reasonable, logical laws based on humanity and fairness.[1] He also sometimes said kind things to me and played with me, welcomed me along on all family vacations and paid for four years of my college, which wasn't cheap. I credit him for that; his positive attributes helped me grow. Yet at the same time he criminalized whole

---

[1] I must make clear, though, that I am highly critical of the American justice system, for a variety of reasons. Here are just a couple of the reasons, apart from the many others I feel: I detest the idea of punishing people for crimes, because I see punishment as barbaric, and also I detest the American concept of being judged by our so-called peers. Are not these "peers" more often than not just emotionally closed-down people wedded to the traumas of their parents? I certainly wouldn't want them judging me.

parts of my healthy self, prosecuting and judging me to the fullest extent of the unspoken laws of his childhood wounds. At times he screamed at me, belittled me, teased me, ignored me and bullied me. And a few times he hit me. But as a child I did not dwell on this, to the point that I, like a good trauma victim, blocked it out. Instead I felt proud of him, because my survival depended on it. He was tall, he was good-looking, he made good money, he was intellectual, he was athletic, he was articulate and he was my dad.

He was the second of two children born to second-generation Jewish immigrants who didn't want him and didn't particularly love him. His mother told one of my father's aunts that he was a mistaken pregnancy whom she would have aborted had it been legal in New York City in 1942. As such, underneath his façade of sophistication and maturity he lacked confidence that he was worthy of love. Hardly a day went by in my childhood where he did not pester my mother to tell him that he was lovable, handsome, intelligent and successful. Deep down he saw himself as the unwanted child who got in the way. And sadly, that was how he often treated me, such that I internalized his attitude and thought there really was something wrong with me.

My mother was her own combination of success and mess. She was a high-functioning, educated, erudite nurse of upper-middle-class, white, Anglo-Saxon stock. In addition to her nursing degree she had a Master's degree in geology and raised me to love the natural world. She taught me to collect and identify fossils and minerals, to catch and pin out butterflies and moths, to do taxidermy and to raise a dozen species of pets. To many of my friends she was the ultimate mother, far beyond normal. And while in a sense she was and I credit her with a lot of my foundation for success in life, behind closed doors she was a woman who had been emotionally warped by her parents, which she expressed, among other ways, through drug use and binge-drinking, both of which she hid and denied. Also, she had porous and sometimes invasive sexual boundaries with me, which set me on a confused sexual path. I have long since realized her behavior toward me was perverted.

My mother remained painfully close to her parents and lived for their approval. Both were high-functioning alcoholics. Her father was a respected psychology professor at Cornell University with a Ph.D. from Harvard, a psychotherapy practice and a penchant for sexually seducing women over whom he had power. From the time I was born he carried on a longstanding romantic affair with one of his former therapy patients, right out in the open, in front of his weak, collusive wife, his emotionally crippled children and his mostly clueless grandchildren. I, however, knew all about this from childhood onward because my mother described it to me in detail, though she did nothing to shield me from it and nothing to confront her parents about its insanity. Few dared challenge my mother's father on anything, much less this ill and sacred cow, because he made it clear that the price for cow-slaughtering was banishment from his life and excision from his will. Both my parents taught me to admire and respect him and strive to win his love. He was the family patriarch; his word was God's word and when he spoke everyone listened. (Incidentally, he was an ordained minister as well, despite being an avowed atheist. I learned to live with this kind of hypocrisy in my childhood in order to survive.)

When I was 23 and my grandfather 83 I confronted him about his romantic affair. That taught me quickly that all my years of investing in bonding with him meant nothing, because he rejected me outright. But by that time I was already well on my way to independence, so his rejection, and the fact that no one in the family came to my defense, didn't kill me to the degree it would have likely killed my mother. And although a few in my family cheered me on silently from the sidelines, not one dared admit this support publicly. It was then that I realized that my actions, from my family's perspective, had begun defining me as a pariah. And, because I didn't crumble—and because the whole experience actually left me with a more conscious and self-reflective relationship with myself—it also started dawning on me that I was stronger than all of them.

Meanwhile, I also have siblings, both biological and step, as my parents are divorced from each other and have since remarried. In preparing this book I have thought long and hard about how much to say about my siblings, and ultimately I have decided to say very little. What little I have written about them I have done in disguised fashion. Although none of my siblings has ever come to my defense during my process of breaking from my parents, let alone joined me, I still do not feel comfortable sharing about them publicly. Although I have had my share of conflict with some of them over the years, none of them were my primary traumatizers. At best they were like peers to me—traumatized by the same people who traumatized me, and if they hurt me (and at points they did, and I did them) it was not in the same league of intensity as those who created us. And I still share a lot of wonderful memories with some of them. In fact, some of them I still love.

As regards my parents, I have decided more often than not to write about them directly, without disguise, both because I often had no better set of illustrations for the points I was making in these pages, and I also wanted to be as transparent as possible — so the reader could better know me. In many ways this has been terrifying. As a child I lived in terror of them destroying me through emotional abandonment if I indulged my secret desire for honesty. This carried over into my adulthood. And although some of this terror still lingers in me, I am stronger now because I have less need for my parents' love and approval. As a child I lived for them to rescue me and as I grew I projected this hope for rescue onto others. Now, through hard inner work, I find that my desire for parental rescue has shrunk because I have instead become, more than ever, my own wounded child's parent, that is, an independent, self-loving adult. And as each month passes I emotionally adopt myself more fully, and mostly I treat myself pretty well.

Yet I want to be clear that I do not write about my parents as a means to seek the flip side of rescue: revenge. Some years back I had an acquaintance who held to the theory that getting revenge on one's family of origin is the best way to heal. I did not agree then and I do not agree now. That's not to say that I've never felt any desire for revenge against my parents; I have. I just don't hold revenge-seeking as a good philosophy for growth. Although I am all for feeling and processing my healthy anger at those who caused me harm, and address this throughout the coming pages, my experience has shown me that seeking revenge on others only hands them my power, keeps me wedded to them and impales me on the hooks of bitterness and resentment. Where is the freedom in that?

I also want to note that in the upcoming pages I have also written about many other people I have known over the years, people who are not part of my family of origin. I did not, however, write about the clients I worked with in therapy. That did not feel right to me. And for the people I did write about, I changed their identifying characteristics, contexts and situations for the sake of anonymity—and where possible asked their permission. Also, sometimes the people I have presented are amalgamations of a variety of people, myself included. But despite the disguises and adjustments, I have tried to remain true to the deeper, universal emotional dynamics of their stories.

SECTION 1: BACKGROUND

Chapter 1: Why the World Resists You

Your desire to break from your parents and their lies is healthy and legitimate. The problem is, the far majority of the world doesn't see it that way. They side with your parents, just as they side with their own parents against themselves and with themselves against their own children. They consider your desire for truth and freedom an uncomfortable thing, perhaps even a sort of moral crime. At the level of their feelings, they say, "You have no right to break from your parents."

But what they are really saying is this: "Your parents own you. They own the essence of your being and the right to define your perceptions of reality. They created you and this makes you theirs until the day they die. By breaking from them you are stealing their property. And stealing is wrong."

To me this sounds like slavery. In the history of America, my homeland, slaves were considered the legal property of their masters. If they escaped they were legally considered thieves for stealing their masters' property. Yet nowadays almost everyone, at least in Western society, considers slavery unethical. The very idea of one human legally owning another disturbs us to the point that we have trouble understanding how a land like America—"with liberty and justice for all"—so few years ago not only allowed it but based its existence on it. Almost no one blames a slave for fleeing the southern plantation on risk of death and traveling to the north. We understand correctly that human relationships are voluntary and that it is wrong for one human to own another and profit from his or her involuntary labor. Even two centuries ago many in the United States understood this and aided escaping slaves through the Underground Railroad. They realized that the real criminals were the owners, not the owned.

But where, two centuries later, is such a movement for those defending the rights of people who want to break from their parents? Where are the safe houses for people like you and me, the newspapers telling our stories, the inflamed rhetoric, the scores of published books, the people willing to break the laws of the land and risk their lives for us and our cause? Instead what we have today is a world that largely blames the victims, obfuscates the issues, defends the perpetrators and looks suspiciously on the agitators, as if there were something inherently wrong with those who promote breaking from the lies of the family, defending the rights of the child and changing society for the better.

At best we have a few people speaking out against the furthest extremes of bad parenting, such as rape of children, female and male genital mutilation, abject neglect and harsh corporal punishment. But what of the milder forms of abuse that most consider healthy and normal or at worst insignificant? Who speaks out against how badly children are affected by conventional religion and education and television? Who speaks out against the negative effects of single parenthood? Who speaks out against the societal glorification of families with multiple children? Who speaks out against parents who take psychiatric medication because they cannot manage their own internal states? And who speaks out against the whole corrupt institution of regular (that is, largely unconscious) people having children?

The movement I espouse, the movement that places the rights of the child, be he full-grown or not, higher than the rights of the parent, is in its infancy. The average person who comfortably sees the evils of slavery would reflexively side with your parents if you broke from them. So many times have I told someone that I have broken from my parents only to have that person ask for no details whatsoever and instead emotionally side with my parents and start arguing with me about why I'm making a mistake and unfairly harming them. This is an issue on which so many people simply lack self-reflection.

To present another metaphor, I have observed that few people (in the Western world, at least) blame a physically abused wife for leaving her sadistic husband. When she stands up for herself, the best of the progressive world encourages and applauds her and sees the logic in trying to give her and her children a safe place to live while she gets back on her feet. Perhaps they will offer her financial resources and legal representation, orders of protection, even a new legal identity. And they provide her endless examples on television and even pop music of other women who have walked the courageous path she is undertaking. The modern world understands that her participation in her marriage is voluntary and if her husband mistreats her she has a right and even responsibility to leave. Yet why doesn't the world understand that these same principles apply to people who want to break from their families of origin?[2]

The answer is sad and simple: the modern world resists supporting people who emotionally or literally break from their parents because almost no one has yet done it to any significant degree. People find it almost impossible to support that which they have not yet done and unconsciously are desperate to do but terrified to admit. The idea is too futuristic and renders them blind with fear.

The reality is that the world is in near-absolute denial of the horror that average parents commit on their children. People have lost their natural-born ability to empathize with children because it was traumatized out of them. They long since lost their connection with the little self they once were and unconsciously still remain. They can literally forget that they were raped, tortured, beaten and neglected, and also, on the milder side of things, can block out their early years of pain, sorrow, rejection, loneliness and hurt. They simply do not remember; this is normal.[3]

---

[2] Here I think of the song the famous Gloria Gaynor song *I Will Survive* (written by F. Perren and D. Fekaris). These lyrics strike me: *"Go on now go walk out the door. Just turn around now 'cause you're not welcome anymore. Weren't you the one who tried to hurt me with goodbye? You think I'd crumble, you think I'd lay down and die."* Can you imagine these lyrics becoming a major pop hit if they were sung by an adult child being harassed by his average parents with whom he'd broken up?

[3] This is why so many people can't remember their childhoods before the ages of five or seven or nine or later… They can't remember not because they weren't gifted with a good memory; they can't remember because it's too painful.

Fully empathizing with life's victims unconsciously terrifies them, because it requires that they face their own inner torment. So instead they displace their empathy onto those who did the traumatizing.[4] They are the hostage who sees the good heart in the kidnapper, the worker who falls in love with the cruel boss and the dog who licks the hand that starves it. And they are the normal children who cannot call either their abusive parents, be they average or extreme, by their real names and instead forever repeat the adage, "They did the best they could."

What Jew in Auschwitz would say that Hitler "did the best he could"? This analogy might seem farfetched, but it isn't for those who know the detailed histories of their own childhood pain at the hands and partially frozen hearts of their parents. And it is even less of a farfetched analogy when one realizes that Hitler and the Germans were themselves only reenacting their own childhood histories of abuse by fomenting the Holocaust. Alice Miller describes this dynamic brilliantly in *For Your Own Good*.[5]

---

[4] Of course, many abused people displace their split-off empathy onto other abused beings, like abused animals or children of famine, but until they can fully empathize with their inner abused selves they will still side to some degree with their traumatizers, and by extension all traumatizers.

[5] It is also interesting to note that Alice Miller, one of the finest psychology writers of the twentieth century, was herself in such profound denial of so many aspects of her own childhood and simply replicated it by treating her own son, Martin Miller, as her personal slave. I thank Martin Miller for his personal communication with me on this subject. See also his book: M. Miller (2013): *Das wahre "Drama des begabten Kindes." Die Tragödie Alice Millers.* Kreuz: Freiburg im Breisgau.

The reason no Jews in Auschwitz defended Hitler is they had no reason to. Jews from Auschwitz could clearly see Hitler as their enemy and any halfway awakened person obviously took their side. Hitler never pretended to be a father figure for the Jews and only stated clearly that he wanted them all dead. And the Jews also had each other, a whole culture, for support and mirroring and witnessing. What culture does a child have for support? The leaders of his culture *are* his parents.

But while parents might, on an emotional level, have some of the same motives as Hitler, their cruel methods and actions are far more private and are infused and thereby disguised with threads of real love and caring. Parents tend to act like "benevolent" kidnappers who induce Stockholm Syndrome in their hostage. Parents only rarely kill their child in body; instead they indoctrinate him into their cult, first by proving themselves absolutely necessary for his survival—which is easy to do with a child— and then by brainwashing him into believing them to be fully on his side. If parents do this job thoroughly, the child buries his pain and rage and suffering and sorrow and grows up to become a clone of them, doing unto his children as was done unto him. And if he does so, he becomes a darling of society and is labeled a good parent. And who will criticize him? He is normal.

And you can bet that unless he heals his own wounds and reconnects with his real self he will be unable to give you much support in breaking deeply from your parents. How could he?

Chapter 2: Breaking Away Is Hell

If breaking from our parents were as simple as cutting them off, blocking their phone calls, changing our email addresses and jumping into a new, better life, a lot more people would do it. Although this pleasant scenario does seem to work for some people — at least on the surface — life for many is not so simple because the work of breaking away can be emotionally arduous and the consequences painful. A key reason is that our personalities formed intertwined with our parents, which allowed their troubled sides to embed themselves deeply and firmly in our psyches.

Although in psychological terms these embedded parts are known as negative parental introjects, or, in shorthand, introjects,[6] I prefer to liken them to warts. A wart is a parasitic virus that embeds itself deeply in your flesh. Your body builds a protective layer of hardened skin around the wart, so much so that the wart can actually seem to be a malformed part of you. But warts are not you; they are your enemy. They drink from your blood supply, they kowtow to a foreign master and they resist like hell coming out. The only difference between warts and introjects is that it's a lot harder to get rid of an introject. You can freeze off a wart; you can't freeze off an introject. Also, some people are so embedded with introjects that they never get a good chance to develop a strong, viable, authentic self at all. Metaphorically speaking, they are more wart than person, yet they don't even know it because they don't know the difference between

---

[6] As much as possible I try in these pages to avoid the use of psychological jargon. My apologies for the occasional exception.

wart and self. Their introjects have almost total control over their thoughts, their self-perceptions and their actions.

As we begin to break free from our parents our introjects come to life. As if commanded by remote control, they turn against our vulnerable, authentic selves with ugly voices, self-doubt and pro-parent thoughts. Some people's introjects pressure them with guilt, as follows: "You are selfish," they might say, "and hurtful to break away. Your parents love you and gave life to you and devoted the best of their energies to you and you *know* that. If it hadn't been for them you wouldn't even be here to think these thoughts. What right do you have to turn your back on them? You really are a *cruel* individual. You hurt them and that's not okay. You should be ashamed of yourself. You deserve whatever punishment they throw at you. Go back to them: you owe them that and you owe yourself that."

Others' introjects try terror tactics: "You cannot make it on your own! You need them! No one really loves you except your parents! No one out in the world even likes you! You will never be close with anyone apart from them! You will die of loneliness without them! You are committing emotional suicide! You are insane for leaving them! Anyone who tells you otherwise is an enemy! Go back to them! Apologize to them! Return to them, fool!"

Not surprisingly, our parents can easily trigger our introjected voices — because our introjected voices are actually the worst of them; they are not us. This triggering can be as simple for them as a phone call, an email, a subtle guilt-trip, a cool tone or a cutting remark. This calls to mind a beautiful old saying about introjects: "Of course your parents can press your buttons: they installed them."

The problem is, in a civilization such as ours, which is largely a massive conglomeration of overlapping family cults upholding the same troubled values, the whole world can press our introjected buttons and send us careening back to our parents. I have met so many people who have broken from their parents on the surface yet, when under pressure, run back to them because they never figured out how to get rid of their introjects. In the past I have done it myself and I still occasionally find myself pressured to do it, especially if I am in an emotionally toxic environment.

As an example, while writing the first draft of this book, I received an email from a middle-aged mother who read my website: "I hope," she wrote, "you can find it in your heart to forgive your mother. And I write this not for her sake, but for yours. Living with the bitterness and anger that you so visibly express is not healthy. I really hope you consider what I'm saying, because you seem like such a genuine and courageous person who could really be very useful to the world."

As another example, some years back, when I worked at a therapy clinic where most of the therapists were parents, I got into a discussion with a colleague, David, who was planning to circumcise his newborn son, his firstborn child, in a Jewish ritual. I tried to convince him not to and took the risk of letting him know that I considered circumcision to be very harmful to infants. He was offended by this and turned my defense of his child back onto me, accusing me of having "an infantile axe to grind with parents."

But it didn't end there. I was later approached by two "senior" therapists, who sided with him.

"Daniel," said one, a mother of three, "he's a new father. It's not respectful to make him feel insecure. Just because you're putting your parents through the spin cycle doesn't mean you have a right to drive a wedge between David and his son."

"It's hard enough as it is to be a new parent," said the other therapist, a father of two, "without everyone giving you their holy opinion on what you're doing wrong. Someday you may have kids and then you'll realize this. In the meantime, I think you might benefit from returning to analysis. You are universalizing your unresolved material."

I tried to point out that David letting his son get circumcised, and not my criticizing it, would drive a wedge between them, but this only made them angry.

"You're too judgmental," said the mother. "Therapists need to be compassionate."

"I'm just trying to side with the child," I said. "And I side with the child inside my clients."

"You miss the point," said the father. "You're just afraid to forgive."

This caused me anxiety. Not only did it kick up the ancient messages embedded in me by my parents—that there was something wrong or defective with me—but it made me feel frightened that I could destroy my career by being so vocal. And my career has been a key ally for me in my path to independence from my family of origin. So I backed off, stopped arguing and let them feel that they had won. But I admit: I hated that.

It is standard operating procedure for normal people to pathologize you if you break from your parents and side with the child. Yet I have become convinced that all people, even the most abusive and conventional, secretly want to side with their own wounded child within. Their wounded inner child is not only the person they love the most in the world but also the person they are most terrified to defend because they learned long ago that when they defended their true inner selves they got rejected in the most painful ways by their parents. Thus, when you side with the child, any true child, you subliminally declare freedom, revolution even, for all wounded inner children. You speak to everyone's heart, including the heart of abusers, which creates terror because it goes against our unconscious training. That is why abusers—and people who side with abusers—resist you. If they didn't resist you then they would have to face the emotional consequences of agreeing with you, which would blow the circuits of their stability.

Your insight threatens people's lack of insight. As those therapists did with me, they will mistake your insight for an attack and then *actually attack you* in order to defend their denial. And the more maturely you develop your logical replies to the insanity they lob at you, the louder and crueler their attacks will be. Perhaps they will call you a crazy or out-of-control person, or a liar or someone with a creative memory. Perhaps they will accuse you of being someone who makes a mountain out of a molehill, a negative person who only remembers the bad things or a sick idealist. Or perhaps they will label you a malingerer, a slanderer or a libelist. I have been labeled all these things. And had I argued further with those therapists, they probably would have gotten me fired.

"After all," I could totally imagine them arguing, "how can we in good conscience allow such a troubled, opinionated, dogmatic, unanalyzed person to be a therapist here? He could really hurt people."

Or perhaps, if your context is a little different, they will call you mentally ill, finding mental health professionals to back them up and brand you delusional, paranoid, borderline, schizophrenic, manic, depressed, psychotic or hysterical. Perhaps they will have you locked up in psychiatric wards, strapped down in four-point restraints and force-injected with antipsychotics. Perhaps they will find ways to get the media on their side. Perhaps they will say you've been dragged into a cult. Or perhaps they will call the police on you and have you arrested and taken to jail. I know people who have experienced all these things for telling the truth.

And perhaps your own body will express your parentally-induced psychological torment. I have seen some people whose physical bodies have manifested their inner conflicts, in all sorts of ways. I have experienced this myself for the last decade, and so will use myself as an example. My physical problems have arisen from a combination of screaming desperation to break fully free from my parents and a simultaneous internalized terror *of* getting away. My first sign of this conflict came with overpowering, migraine or migraine-like headaches that exploded in the middle of the night while I was sleeping. Their pain was so horrendous I would run to the bathroom to vomit. I tried journaling to help myself get at the root of my feelings and twice while journaling I unraveled the emotional knot of the headache and wept in grief and empathy for myself, evaporating the headache immediately. Most other times I couldn't access the nugget and instead suffered for hours or took pain pills.

My headaches finally went away after about a year but the source of emotional conflicts causing them did not, leading my body to express my buried horror in a new way: ulcerative colitis, that is, inflammation of the large intestine. In many ways this was even worse. For five years I lived with chronic, bloody diarrhea, a terror of going outside for fear of bathroom accidents, an inability to eat almost anything normal and the excruciatingly painful side effect of kidney stones, for which I had to have surgery. It was not fun. Not knowing what else to do aside from continuing to heal emotionally and refusing to heed my introjects and return to my parents, I took the pills my doctors prescribed, to no avail. They said I was "an irregular case." I tried to explain to them that my journaling and life experience demonstrated to me that my problem was emotionally caused and that there was good scientific evidence showing how intimately the brain, the emotions and the gut are interconnected, but they had no clue what I was talking about and ignored me. I would have gotten more empathy from a witch doctor than a modern "scientifically-trained" medical doctor.

Only in the last three years—years of profound distance from my parents—has the colitis eased, such that I no longer take any pills and have almost no symptoms. In some ways this has been a miracle, because none of the doctors predicted it, much less predicted that it would happen while simultaneously quitting all their prescribed drugs. But I am not fully healed. Physically the colitis has been replaced by vitiligo (disappearance of pigment on the skin of my hands and feet). I assume that this too is temporary and I only wonder what is next. I think it will reflect my inner journey, but I cannot predict how, because frankly, very little of this has been terribly predictable to me. Meanwhile, I don't want to make myself sound insane with physical symptoms, but this has been my history. The reality, though, is that this insanity was implanted in me by my family system and my physical symptoms are only manifestations of its eruption through various lenses of my body.

And while this has been hell for me and for others whose similar stories I have heard, it is, as odd as this might sound, a hell I personally welcome. Deep inside I know this to be true. Slowly and progressively it has been saving my life.

Chapter 3: Parents Avoid Responsibility

Our society allows parents great liberty in not having to take responsibility for the disturbed things they do to their children. Although this is slowly shifting, such that parents are prosecuted more nowadays for sexual abuse and extreme violence, these crimes are just the extreme tip of the abuse iceberg. Child abuse happens when people in power do anything that harms the emotional self of the child. By this definition, 99 percent of the iceberg still remains hidden under water, unacknowledged by almost anyone and perfectly legal. And if you defend the abused child in these unacknowledged situations, society as a whole will blame you. After all, most people are in such a trance that they don't even realize that children have much of an emotional self. All they see clearly is children with bodies that can be bruised and genitals that can be violated. And they only defend, if they do any defending at all, that which they can see clearly.

Recently I was on the subway in New York City sitting across from a young couple and their crying three-year-old son. The mother told the boy, "Shut your damn mouth right now. I've heard enough crying out of you." When he kept crying, she rolled up her eyes and said, "Fine, you go on crying, but when we get home you're gonna go right to bed and that's all there is." The child's eyes grew wide with fear and he struggled to stifle his tears. Meanwhile, his father sat on the other side of him, uninterested, and said nothing. And no one on the train said anything either.

I considered my options. My first option was to say what I was feeling in hopes of having them take responsibility for their actions.

My proposed words: "Stop abusing that child. First, he's crying for a reason. Obviously he's upset. The appropriate response is to hold him and hug him and talk gently with him. Second, you, his mother, are denying his feelings by ordering him to stop. That's abusive. You should respect his feelings. Third, you just threatened him with physical isolation for not following your orders. That is torture, which is seriously abusive. He needs physical closeness, not isolation. Fourth, you, his father, did absolutely nothing to defend him. That's neglect, which is abusive as well. He needs a father who stands up for him, otherwise he will have a very hard time learning to stand up for himself. You parents need serious help, because you yourselves are both wounded children and have no right to have an actual child under your care."

The result of this option: the mother would likely have cursed me out for not "minding my business" and the father might have physically threatened me (or worse) for "disrespecting his child's mother." And it's doubtful anyone on the train would have defended me and perhaps someone else would have joined the parents in confronting me. After all, my reality-based definition of abuse threatens to rock the apple cart of society's denial. Also, it's highly unlikely these parents would become *less* abusive toward their child as the result of my intervention. They actually probably would have punished him *more* for it. That is the sick privilege of parenthood.

My second option was to say nothing and log the incident in my mental database. That is what I did. I stared powerlessly at the little boy, struggling to make eye contact with him in the useless hope that somehow he would know that someone out there understood what was happening and cared. I also found myself contemplating his life in fifteen or twenty years. After all, his abuse won't just go away. He will replicate it somehow. In this vein, more than likely twenty years earlier I was watching his parents, then little children themselves, get treated in the same perfectly legal way on the subway.

I see this type of parental behavior all over. Before I became a psychotherapist I played music for pre-Kindergarteners in a New York City public school. One season of that job was enough for me, because, among other reasons, many parents blamed the teachers and the school for everything and no one stood up to them. No matter that their kids came to school hungry from having not been properly fed, tired from having stayed up all night, inappropriately dressed because of parental neglect and violent and hypersexualized from the things they watched on television and saw their families do.

Their kid couldn't do puzzles? According to the parent, that meant the teacher was inept. Their kid couldn't get along with classmates? The school psychologist was incompetent. Their kid fought on the playground? The school lacked proper supervision. Although I don't entirely defend the school, because I'm no fan of schools in general and because many of the staff, even those who gave it their all, were burned out, it amazed me how little the world required that parents take responsibility for their actions and for the consequences of their actions.

As another story of parents who eschew responsibility, a Chicago therapist I know told me about her thirty-year-old client, Kristin. Kristin felt bereft about a recent romantic breakup and anxious about ongoing conflict with her parents. Because of the conflict she had not spoken with them in several months and was considering making a more permanent break. Kristin was an only child who came from a home in which her father occasionally slapped her mother and her mother emasculated him by having extramarital affairs. Her parents had regularly dragged Kristin into their battles, each trying to win her to their respective side with enticements and each growing cold toward her if she took the side of the other. As a result, Kristin had felt devastated or simply miserable for much of her childhood, which had prompted her parents to take her to a psychiatrist for antidepressants, which, incidentally, they both took. Kristin, however, had adamantly refused medication, causing them both to torment her further for "rebelling" and "refusing the help she needed."

Kristin saw the therapist for three sessions spread over six weeks, despite agreeing to meet weekly. She skipped three of the sessions without notice and came late to two of the three she made. She admitted that she felt ambivalent about therapy because of having been forced to see the psychiatrist as a child. Despite this, she did do some exploration in her sessions, noting the similarly between her ex-boyfriend and her parents.

Like them, her ex-boyfriend had demeaned her, been volatile toward her, tried to control her and stored up anything personal she shared with him to use against her later.

The result of this story is that after the third session Kristin had a reunion with her boyfriend, had sex with him, then immediately afterward had a fight with him, at which point he left her once again. For her that was the last straw. She climbed onto the roof of her apartment building and jumped, committing suicide.

I share this story because afterward her parents sued the therapist for malpractice. Although they set Kristin up for her dysfunctional adulthood, they took no responsibility. And a jury agreed with them, awarding them a $250,000 judgment against the therapist's malpractice insurance. The reason: based on Kristin's diagnosis of "major depressive disorder" the therapist had not adequately pressured her to go to a psychiatrist for a medication evaluation! That is, the therapist had not taken up Kristin's parents' call-to-arms to follow their path and medicate away the very feelings that they induced in her.[7]

---

[7] Although this is a slightly fictionalized case example, for very real facts on the dangers of psychiatric drugs, please see Robert Whitaker's *Anatomy of an Epidemic: Magic Bullets, Psychiatric Drugs, and the Astonishing Rise of Mental Illness in America* (Crown Books, 2011). Also, for a good start to see how psychiatric medication can induce both depression and suicidality, see Peter Breggin's books: (1) *Medication Madness: The Role of Psychiatric Drugs in Cases of Violence, Suicide and Murder* (St. Martin's Press, 2008); and (2) *Toxic Psychiatry: Why Therapy, Empathy, and Love Must Replace the Drugs, Electroshock, and Biochemical Theories of the 'New Psychiatry'* (St. Martin's Press, 1991).

Rather than outing Kristin's abusive parents for robbing her of her authentic self, the legal system, part of the fraternity of parents, compensated them for having "been robbed" of their daughter. But this analysis is taboo. After all, by conventional societal standards and even by psychiatric standards they didn't abuse her at all. In fact, by psychiatric standards, which arise from the mores of our pro-family, denial-based society (and the money of Big Pharma), they were "the bereaved," they were "her best allies," they had "her best interest at heart" and "they loved her unconditionally." And damn the truth.

I went red when I heard this story. But since my rage had nowhere to be expressed, I diverted it into a fantasy in which the devastated therapist, who, in two hours of sitting with Kristin saw her childhood dynamics more clearly than her parents ever had, would sue the parents! She would sue them for having destroyed their child and for having indirectly traumatized the therapist herself. And she would win. But she would not keep the money and might not even sue for money at all. Instead she would sue to set the record straight. She would sue for some measure of justice for Kristin, as if such a thing were even possible.

But with our world in such denial this could never happen. Our world believes that except in certain extreme cases parents are to be protected at all costs.[8] Our world considers parents' past abuses of their children to be of little or no significance. Our world believes that children go unaffected by the average horrors of their environment or they consider children to be "resilient." If only they were so resilient. Children only *seem* resilient to people who, because of their own unresolved and unacknowledged traumas, lack empathy for them.

Society largely offers parents a free ticket to abuse their child as long as they don't break a few basic rules regarding extreme sexual or physical abuse. Just to make clear what I mean, I will list and flesh out twelve conventionally acceptable forms of child abuse, each of which will traumatize him or her:

(1) Lying to a child, which sends the child this message: "Your perceptions are invalid. In order for me to love you, you have to trust my dishonesty more than you value your emotional connection with truth."

(2) Manipulating a child through ultimatums such as the silent treatment, which sends this message: "Although you need me to love you, I

---

[8] In Japan some railway companies sue the parents or families of people who commit suicide by having jumped in front of trains, but they sue not based on psychology or for justice for the victim but instead to retrieve money the company loses from temporary closures of its rail lines. [See: French, Howard W. (June 6, 2000). "Kunitachi City Journal; Japanese Trains Try to Shed a Gruesome Appeal" (*The New York Times, Health Section*).] Also, there was a case in Germany in which a traumatized train conductor sued the parents of a young man who committed suicide by having jumped in front of his train. [See: July 28, 2011: Train Driver Sues Parents of Suicide Victim. *The Local: Germany Edition*.]

don't. In fact, you are so worthless that it's okay for me to torture you. Submit or I'll reject you. Your desires to dialogue, self-express and be heard mean nothing."

(3) Emotionally leaning on a child, which says: "I won't parent you unless you parent me first. Take care of me. I created you to love me. All love is conditional, except of course yours for me, which must remain unconditional."

(4) Using double binds, that is, two simultaneous but mutually conflicting messages or commands, which says: "You're damned if you do and damned if you don't. It's lose-lose for your authenticity and win-win for my dishonesty. So submit!"

(5) Emotionally bullying or teasing a child, which says: "Your existence bothers me, your emotions get in my way, your boundaries mean nothing and hurting you makes me feel good."

(6) Subtly sexualizing a child or commenting negatively on his or her looks, which says: "Your value to me, and thus to the world, is not as a centered, real, true, respected, emotional human being, but as a sexual object for adults."

(7) Not following through on your word, which says: "You cannot count on me and nothing you do or feel will change that. You and your feelings are not that important to me."

(8) Demanding perfection from a child, which says: "You are not allowed to make mistakes, you are not allowed to experiment and you are not allowed to grow."

(9) Failing to be a mature role model for a child, which says: "Although I am the most important person in your world, I have little of value to teach you. Thus, if you want to become a great person you will have to reject me, which, of course, is impossible because you need me too much. You are trapped."

(10) Having a child put on psychiatric medication, which says: "You are inherently flawed and only an outside substance can manage you. The problem is within you. Not only are we, your parents, not the problem, but even if we were we will never change."

(11) Using a child as a pawn in a divorce or custody battle, which says: "You are a tool by which I can act out my immaturity, rage and selfishness. I don't care about you or your other parent. I am not committed to you and never was. You are worthless."

(12) Ripping a child out of his or her social network through moving from location to location, which says: "I don't care about the life you've built because my life is more important. Your stability is not my priority and your attachments don't count. Your terror of starting over is not my primary concern."

And we wonder why our world is so sick?

Chapter 4: Suicide Protects Parents

An adult child who commits suicide threatens parents much less than one who breaks away and gets real. An adult child who commits suicide dies with many or all of his family's secrets hidden, whereas one who gets real rips the truth wide open. Although Kristin, mentioned in the previous chapter, probably did trigger a significant amount of pain in her parents by killing herself, she would have triggered a lot more had she broken away from them and outed their lies by healing from the abuse they inflicted on her. And I purposefully use the word "triggered," not "caused," because Kristin did not *cause* her parents' pain. Her parents' own abusive parents caused their pain. Kristin just helped bring this historical pain to the surface, and had her parents nurtured their own healing orientation they would have used this pain to heal. But instead they used it to cement their denial into place, for which they were rewarded financially.

The reason I return to Kristin's story is that I find the dynamics underlying her suicide to be universal. I have never met suicidal people, including chronically ill elderly people who want to commit suicide due to physical pain, for whom I could not say, once I got a chance to know their deeper story, that their suicidality was not profoundly motivated by their history of childhood abuse. In fact, people have no other *more* motivating factor to kill themselves than a history of having been abused by their parents, that is, a history of having been already partially emotionally maimed by their parents.

Suicide is a logical but unconscious reenactment of the psychological homicide committed on children by their parents. But suicide is only a logical reenactment by a child who never became able to face the emotional reality of what he went through. For people who break from their parents and develop a strong relationship with their authentic selves, replicating by suicide the horror of being crushed by their parents no longer makes sense. If we have the good fortune to break from our parents, we instead grow more loving toward ourselves each day. This becomes our new template for behavior. But if we don't break from our parents, and break deeply from them, we stay trapped in the lies. And then we can never become uncrushed.

In this vein, I often hear parents say that they would die for their child. Essentially never, though, do I hear them say that they would *get real for their child*, because that doesn't cross their mind; they have no template for it.

Instead they generally say one of the following pat statements, which I will translate into reality.

They say: "I would sacrifice my life for my child."

My translation: "If my child sacrifices his authentic self for my unconscious needs and accepts my distorted point of view about him, I will protect what's left of him. That is, if my child stops battling against my abuse and buries his authenticity, I will consider him of such high value that I will sacrifice my life, which I don't consider to be of particularly high value, for him."

They say: "I love my child unconditionally."

My translation: "I am unconditionally enmeshed with my child. That is, I am so mixed up in my sense of who I am and who my child is and what our mutual boundaries are as separate individuals that I mistake enmeshment for love."

They say: "I love my child even more than I love myself."

My translation: "I so thoroughly don't know my real self and real motives and real feelings that I delude myself into believing that I am totally on my child's side, even though I significantly crushed my child's real self and I am actually on the side of the abusive parents who crushed me."

And they conclude with the following: "You never really know what love is until you have a child."

And here is how I translate this: "I abandoned my inner child because my parents forced me to; because of that I have no clue what true love is, which of course suggests that I should never have had children. And the fact that you're hinting at how emotionally ignorant I am causes me, in self-soothing protection of my ignorance, to label you the ignorant one."

Conditional love is the standard of modern parental love. As such, when a child does not do what his parents want him to do or even demand that he does, they stop loving him. And often they actively hate him—and sometimes they even admit it. Examples of extreme cases of this admitted hatred come when parents disown their children for becoming gay or for joining a different religion or for marrying or having children with someone of a different race or ethnicity. And in some places in the world parents simply kill their female children because they don't meet the condition of being male.

But the example of children breaking from sophisticated parents interests me more, because it highlights how incipient murderousness exists where we would least expect it. Here I think of my friend Tracy. She came from a professional, educated family, she received many of the good perks of a white, middle-class life, yet somehow she had the passion and wherewithal to break the trance into which her parents had put her. Her parents were masters of manipulation, double binds and the silent treatment and by the time Tracy was in college she started to talk openly about this with her peers. Her parents tried to silence her through various means, including telling lies about her, besmirching her good name and labeling her mentally ill, all of which failed. She only used their cruelty to grow more real and to break further away. I recently asked her if she thought they would be happier if she killed herself.

"Are you kidding?" she replied. "Of course they would! Absolutely. I am destroying their fragile little world of lies and control and they hate me for it. By getting real I force them to face how dishonest they are and how deficient they were as parents. They've put a ton of energy into denying it and it would spare them a lot of work if I just died or killed myself."

"So which do you think they'd prefer?" I asked. "You dying or you killing yourself?"

"Killing myself," she answered. "That would demonstrate 'proof' that I was mentally ill, which is the bill of goods they've been trying to sell everyone anyway. If I killed myself they would start spinning to everyone how much they'd always loved me and how horrible they felt about my 'poor, tragic fate.' But the truth is, from the minute I started getting real about how lousy they were as parents they didn't care about me or my fate. They only cared about my well-being when I was playing their game of denial. After I quit the game they wanted me dead."

Tracy's story reminds me in some ways of my own. I have come to accept that at various points in my breaking away process my parents would have likely been relieved if I had committed suicide. It has certainly not been easy for them to have a son who publicly labels them abusers. Yet their desire for the easy path has not been my responsibility. On the contrary, it was the essence *of* my problem! Their desire for the easy path was what, in no small part, led them to abuse me in the first place: the more traumatized I was the less I challenged them. And the converse holds true as well: the more real and mature and life-loving I have become the more dangerous I become to their denial. I write books such as these, whereas dead men labeled "mentally ill" cannot tell the truth.

As a speaker on the radical psychology circuit about recovery from psychosis without medication, I not infrequently meet parents whose so-called "mentally ill" children have committed suicide. Many of these parents have become activists against psychiatry and speak about the horrors psychiatry did to their children. Although psychiatry *is* unethical and regularly abuses people, sometimes to the extreme, the way that psychiatry treats patients is an extension of the way parents-in-denial treat their children. Psychiatry almost always fails to look at problems in a greater context, and instead tries to "treat" the consequence of the problem, and even medicalizes these consequence as symptoms, which it then attacks with pills and hospitals and the like. But if parents didn't abuse their children there would be no psychiatry at all. The two function very similarly, with their lies, their coercion, their demand for acquiescence and, not surprisingly, their trail of harm.[9]

Although the circuit on which I speak is radical, because the mental health field is largely so blind to the obvious, the subject about which I write here is presently a quantum leap beyond radical; it is taboo. When I think back on the last ten or so conferences I attended, I conclude that if I addressed this subject matter there I would not be invited back. Rarely does anyone even come close to speaking about it. Instead I hear the parent advocates,

---

[9] A person or group that is antipsychiatry, however, is by no means pro-healing. The troubled mores of the Church of Scientology proves that well enough.

who are sometimes invited and paid, give idealized lectures about how much they "loved their 'mentally troubled' child," how "wonderful" their relationship was with their child, how they devoted their lives to their child, how their child was a "great soul touched by mental distress" and how devastating the suicide was *for them as parents*.

I almost never hear a single one of them, except in rare, private, confidential, one-on-one moments of deep anguish even approach the topic of taking responsibility for their actions. And these moments of exception come only when the parents feel unconditionally supported by a nurturing ally who empathizes primarily with the child within them and only secondarily with their actual child who has committed the act of self-murder. Simply put, when these parents are on their own and not feeling support for their own wounded inner child, they do not empathize with their dead child's point of view—and cannot even if they wanted to. They don't have the internal structure to do it. It's too much of a stretch for them—even intellectually. Instead I hear them speak through the lens of their unconscious defenses: about how "an important part of a parent's healing process is to get over the guilt" and "the necessity of embarking on the process of radical forgiveness." And then I observe the bulk of the parents and the denial-laden therapists and the mental health "consumers" in the audience applaud the speaker's "courage" and "maturity" and "devotion."

But I do not applaud. And although I don't believe in heaven, I know that if there were a heaven the speaker's child, who committed suicide first and foremost because of the torture inflicted on her by her parents, from which she never figured out how to escape, would not applaud either. Instead she would scream down the following from her cloud above: "Go to hell, Mom, you hypocrite! Your parents destroyed you, then you probably more than half-unknowingly destroyed me, and now you're milking gold out of me by making yourself out to be my savior. I know you are suffering from all that has happened, but how about start by taking responsibility for your own life and your own actions instead? You screwed up and my screwup was that I failed to figure out how to break away from you! Oh, and from Dad too! Because he's half-responsible for the damages of my childhood."

Chapter 5: Do Your Parents Owe You?

If you are a child, your parents owe you a lot. They owe you nurturance, time, respect, guidance, consistency, loyalty, stability, healthy community, money, food, shelter and the model of a healthy relationship between them as mother and father, partner and partner. They owe you their conscious presence, without the influence of drugs or alcohol or psychiatric medication. They owe you the ability to sense your age-appropriate needs and to be able to meet them. They owe you the most mature, emotionally available, insightful, loving parents you can possibly have. When they had sex to create you, they made a contract with the new life that was you. The small print on the contract stipulated that in every area of parenting they committed to doing a great job. And if they failed in any area, they failed to live up to the contract.

This, however, highlights the contract's unfair parts: first, that there is no way for you to collect for the damages they inflicted on you, and second, that if you are an adult they no longer owe you anything. If they failed you, and more so *where* they failed you, it is now your responsibility to clean up the mess. In short, even though they broke it, it's your job to fix it.

The question is, when does your adulthood begin?

If we speak of physiological adulthood, which is marked by the passing through puberty and the ability to procreate, then some as young as eight or nine are technically adults. If we speak about emotional adulthood, most people remain partial children their whole lives, until death. However, for the purposes of this book I define the age of adulthood as beginning roughly in your early twenties, give or take a few years. This is the time in which you gain the social, occupational and psychological capacity to become your own functional, independent person and in essence to receive the responsibility for becoming your own parent. The job of raising the remaining childish and adolescent parts of yourself now becomes yours and no one else's. It becomes your job to heal your wounds and learn to live maturely.

The reason I address this subject is because many people in their twenties or thirties or forties or beyond hear parts of my point of view, misconstrue my meaning and misapply it to their lives. They think that because I am so "harsh" on parents and because I so strongly side with the child that I feel their parents still owe them something. This could not be further from the truth.

Consider the example of Paul, a 35-year-old man who recently sent me a long email detailing his story. He'd read some of my website and felt he'd found an ally in me. Paul slept in his parents' furnished basement, didn't work, lived off an allowance they gave him and spent most of the day smoking marijuana, playing video games and surfing the web. (I grant this is a rather extreme case, but so be it.) He was rightly furious at his parents for having destroyed his childhood, as I trusted his description of what they did to him decades earlier, yet he felt they owed him "compensation."

He wanted my advice on how to go about getting it. He was offended when I replied, gently, that although I trusted that they certainly had set him up for a life of misery they no longer owed him anything. Now it was his responsibility to quit smoking weed, get a job, stop taking their money, move out and start taking his life seriously.

The same applies to me. Parenting myself is my job. It is no longer my parents' job or anyone else's job. It is not my friends' jobs and if I have a girlfriend it's not her job. And if I have children it's certainly not their job. Once we become chronological adults we can't look outside ourselves to find others, even therapists, to tend to our unresolved childhood needs. If we do, we, like Paul, secretly stay children and don't evolve optimally. That's not to say that I in my adulthood haven't had my share of emotionally-charged fantasies about my parents or other parental surrogates rescuing me, because I have and still have that capacity, but that doesn't make them appropriate fantasies.

Meanwhile, on the other hand, not infrequently I get emailed or called by parents themselves wondering what *they* owe their angry, grown-up, demanding and often seemingly helpless children. They see me as one who speaks in a language similar to that of their children but with the twist of a "professional" perspective. The general feedback I provide is that they should do what they can to help their adult child transition to proper adulthood. That generally includes finding ways of gradually and respectfully withdrawing the support, be it material or emotional or both, to which they have made their child addicted. This often requires delicateness if it is to be done with respect. Sometimes they may have to increase their support in one area while they decrease it in another. For instance, I know some parents who have withdrawn their emotional support while temporarily boosting the financial and others who have withdrawn the financial while temporarily boosting the emotional. Rarely is this either simple or easy.

In many cases the inappropriate support they provide *has* actually been a form of metaphorical compensation for that which they failed to provide emotionally when he was young. Now this support is misplaced, age-inappropriate and damaging because it sends their child the age-old message that he is incompetent to figure out life himself. And the longer they send him that message the more likely he will be not just to believe he is incompetent but actually to become incompetent. All too often it is a self-fulfilling prophecy. In other cases they unconsciously provide him support with the intent of keeping him addicted to them for life because they themselves are terrified of being alone. And in other cases they are inappropriately giving him that which they themselves fantasized getting from their own parents but never got. And sometimes they are doing a simultaneous combination of all of these.

Yet the bottom line "advice"—or perhaps guidance—I give to parents, which scant few can take, is that their responsibility is to grow. It is their responsibility to study themselves, to be rigorously honest with themselves about their own motives, to heal their own inner wounds of childhood and to learn proper boundaries. Part of this involves breaking from their own parents, whether or not their parents are already dead. And then (though usually I never get this far with parents, because this gets too advanced) it becomes vital that parents take responsibility for the inappropriate things they did to their children, first by acknowledging to themselves what ancient wounds within them caused them to make the errors they made and then by resolving the wounds. This is quite a task.

If my own parents had followed this advice, or at least seriously attempted it and continued to work at it, I'd probably be closer with them now. After all, instead of being impediments to my inner journey they would have come much closer to being allies. And I'm not one to discount anyone as a potential ally. But at the same time, I am not sure how close I ever would be with my parents, even if they devoted themselves optimally to growth, in part because there's too much water under the bridge and in part because I don't have the imagination to picture being very close with them. The idea of them devoting themselves to healing seems farfetched to me. But I do acknowledge that some degree of increased closeness could be possible, even now, after all these years. And I think this is possible with most parents and their children, given time and dedication from the parents' side.

Yet when it comes to heeding my "advice," most parents do the opposite at the first sign of conflict with their children. They stop studying themselves, they batten the hatches of their inner worlds, they violate boundaries and often they regress into a victim mentality in which they see their children as perpetrators. At other times they do the mirror image of this and retreat into pity for their children, thus placing themselves in the ludicrous and untenable position of benevolent saviors. And commonly parents want their children "fixed," that is, they want all their family problems swept under the rug of normalcy and denial.

As I mentioned in a previous chapter, before I was a therapist I worked as a musician with children and developed a reputation for having a talent with young people. When I transitioned careers many parents wanted to refer me their children as psychotherapy clients. The problem was that I didn't want to see children in therapy because I could see that it was the parents who more appropriately belonged there. It was the parents' responsibility to change. What I learned quickly, though, was that rarely did the parents want to come. Most actively resisted it and even found themselves insulted that I would suggest such a thing. Again and again I heard the following, sometimes with annoyance at me, sometimes with true bewilderment and sometimes with both: "But *I* don't have the problem. I'm fine. My *child* has the problem."

And few of the parents who did come had much capacity to change. Most instead wanted to place all the burden of the pathology and the obligation to compromise, that is, to buckle under, on the child, neither of which, of course, were appropriate. And few if any of them really, at a deep level, wanted their child to heal, that is, to do any deeper inner work than simply achieve "symptom relief." Deeper healing would have threatened them worse than anything. They even taught us along these lines in graduate school.

"Be careful," my professors and supervisors told us, "of siding too strongly with the child therapy patient against his or her parents. It's a major mistake that new therapists make. They identify *with* the child and *against* the parent. This makes for problems, not the least of which is that the parents will yank their kid out of therapy the minute they get wind of what's happening behind closed doors."

Instead they taught us that apart from cases of severe physical or sexual abuse (in which we should contact the police or child protective services) our job was to be unethical and mirror society by siding with the parents, sometimes even in family therapy with the whole family there. At best we might be allowed to listen quietly to a child's misery and provide him weak, powerless, ineffectual witnessing.

Had they been ethical they would have taught us not only that therapy with kids is *itself* largely unethical but that the root unethical juggernaut is unconscious parenting. But how could they tell us that, considering the majority of them were unconscious parents themselves and the rest just sided deeply with their own parents?

Yet what if we, that is, you or I, did have parents who were optimally focused on healing their own personal wounds? How would they treat us now that we are adults?

The answer is simple: with extreme boundaries, that is, with respect.

For example, here is how a healthy parent might talk with an adult child like Paul: "Son, I screwed up. I screwed up royally when you were the most vulnerable and now I will carry that to my grave. And part of the horrible burden I must carry for gaining the awareness of how much I screwed up is that I now recognize how very little I can do for you. In the coming weeks or months or years I will no longer be able give you money or take care of you in any way, because that only cripples you further. The only thing I will be able to give you is the model of an adult who strives, with all his being, to heal his own childhood wounds. I am in the process of breaking from my own parents and discovering who I really am deep inside. That is my mission. As such, I now respect you as a fellow, voluntary individual on this planet, but I will no longer pretend to be your nurturing parent, because I can no longer be that. That time is over. I now realize that you are on your own. And I truly wish you well on your journey."

An adult child expecting parental compensation would likely feel a range of emotions at hearing such a speech. Perhaps he would feel insulted or hurt or shocked or afraid. Perhaps he would feel devastating lonely. Perhaps he would feel cheated and murderously angry, mistakenly considering his parent a sadist, because many sadistic parents do give speeches along the lines of "toughen up, kid, time to fly the nest." Or perhaps he would just want to die.

Ironically, these would be the very feelings he has kept buried for his whole life. These feelings are the logical consequences of being an abused, neglected child. And as we mature we realize that these feelings are our allies. They guide us forward. They tell us the truth about our history and lead us directly to our authentic self. They give us the opportunity to see what we lack inside and they give us the rudiments of the plan for how to construct lives that can provide what we are lacking.

This seeming rejection by the mature parent is a vitally important dose of reality, because it finally sends us off in a healthy direction: away from them. The problem is, most parents are far too immature to treat their adult children this way, and too terrified as well. First, most could never admit what they really did to their children. And second, even if they could admit it most wouldn't dare want to provoke their children to such wild feelings. Instead they want to keep their adult children close to them, as pets.

But children are not pets. They are wild animals. They owe their parents nothing. Thus, the children of healthy parents grow up, leave home forever and find healthy ways to function in the wilds of the world. It is only the broken pets and broken zoo animals of the human world who are afraid to wander out from their open-doored cages and test the realities of real life. The world might congratulate the broken child who grows up and spends his life tending to his parents, but this only shows how sick the world is. And if parents are afraid to set their children free, then they admit through their behavior that they have failed as parents.

But as a final point here, what about reparations, that is, compensation for damages done in childhood? I have had some people suggest that this would be fair. Perhaps, for example, parents could pay for their troubled adult child's therapy. Or perhaps a father who long ago broke his child's teeth—or ruined them through feeding him sugary junk food—could now pay for adult dental care. Is this okay? I sit on the fence here, but if I were to climb off the fence I would climb away from reparations—and climb toward getting away from our parents and learning to sort out our own lives and our own problems ourselves, through non-parental means. Again: ultimately we as adults become responsible for ourselves. And we have within us the tools to do it. Seeking our parents' help is a slippery slope that all too easily repositions us in the role of a child. And to me it's not worth it.

Chapter 6: Forgiveness

I often find it difficult to discuss breaking up with parents without someone bringing up the subject of forgiveness. Personally I don't find the two subjects inherently related, but in a society like ours that puts so much pressure on children to forgive their parents, somehow the two have become blended, like a drink concoction of fruit and poison. But why is my point of view so strong on this subject?

My main personal reason is that the pressure to forgive has been repeatedly used as a weapon against me — by my parents, my grandparents, by other parents, by friends who are parents, by non-parent adults wedded to their parents, by religion, by most psychology books, by many therapists, by school and by the television. The list could go on and on. The conventional point of view is hard to escape. Our society considers forgiveness to be healthy and considers not forgiving to be a sort of "sin," something to be ashamed of or hide or get over. So many supposedly great leaders and gurus say things like, "Forgiveness is the root of healing. You cannot heal (or be happy) until you begin by forgiving." And the crowd swoons and chants and people feel blissfully happy — on the surface. And those of us living in a deeper realm of consciousness feel more alone than ever.

I find it important to start by defining forgiveness. The dictionary defines forgiveness as "the act of excusing a mistake or offense."[10] In the context

---

[10] See: http://www.wordnet-online.com/forgiveness.shtml

of parental abuse and breaking away from parents, I prefer to call forgiveness by its real name: *dissociation*. I define dissociation as the act of denying the horror you experienced, burying your authentic self, sacrificing your well-deserved rage and pain, curtailing your grieving process, closing your eyes to reality, putting your head in the sand, pretending everything's "just fine," taking the side of the perpetrator, going numb and squelching all urges to heal. In all my experience, when people say they forgive their parents they're dissociating. They give up on their true selves.

But, for the sake of argument, could it ever be healthy to forgive one's parents, if, let's say, one's parents have really taken full responsibility for their actions, healed their own inner childhood wounds that caused them to commit their errors and devoted their lives to stopping such offenses? My answer is "no." I still find the idea of forgiveness irrelevant, because nothing excuses the horrors of the past. There is no excuse. Yes, there is understanding, yes, there can be healing, and yes, perhaps certain degrees of respectful reconnection can potentially become possible, assuming that the child had also healed these wounds, but I've never seen parents do this level of healing. In fact, not even close. I don't know a single set of parents, or even an individual parent, who deeply even understands what he or she has done. This might sound extreme, but this is my experience: the denial of most parents is profound. Most, even the healthiest, simply have little clue what damage they've done, and, like a weak filament in a lightbulb, burn out if someone explains it to them. It's just too painful, too overwhelming, too sad and too contrary to their consciousness. Yes, sometimes parents, to their credit, do understand certain aspects of what they've done, but not the whole picture. For this reason I prefer to strip away the veneer, shelve the gurus and their books and talk about dissociation instead.

But to backtrack a little, there is a good reason so many people strive to forgive their parents: when they were children, *not* forgiving their parents, that is, not dissociating from parental abuse, had serious emotional consequences. Children who do not dissociate actually have to feel their appropriate responses to that which was done to them. They feel their sorrow, their dashed hopes, their misery, their upwelling grief, their rage, their sickening fury, their desire to kill, their desire to cry, their desire for justice, and their burning desire to be heard. And if they feel these things their parents will in some way banish them from the family system. This highlights the value in dissociating: it provides a lifeline for the abused child to stay connected to his abusive parents. And this is a profound template for living, for surviving. Most never break from it, even after their parents are dead.

This template also provides perks outside the family system. If you are an adult who seems to have forgiven, you are allowed to join the cult of other adults who also seem to have forgiven, the conventional cult of doublespeak known as "maturity." It is comforting to join a whole world of people who embrace you for being like them. It is pleasurable and makes social life smooth and certainly easier, unless, of course, you feel that desperate urge to get real at all costs. Then you will realize that no matter how supposedly forgiving are the people you once called your fellows, you are a homeless outsider. Your insight into the truth makes you a reject. It is a sad irony that it is considered an unforgivable sin amongst those who worship false forgiveness for you to refuse to forgive your parents. You are the gust of north wind that topples their house of cards.

Meanwhile, how, I wonder, can it be possible for us to let people off the hook for crushing us when we've never even had the chance to heal from our damage? Actually it isn't possible. Nevertheless, our species has attempted to build a society around excusing parental perpetrators. Yet so few see how insane this is. What we need to do instead is to grow and heal and process our wounds, parental pain be damned. Or to put it more gently: our parents' pain is not our concern. We can't excuse anyone and shouldn't try: instead we need to study ourselves, learn what was done to us, grieve our wounds and perhaps at some point, if it causes us no harm and enhances our growth, even explore the histories of those who damaged us: to discover their motivations. But attempting to excuse them only sends us in the wrong direction.

As an analogy, should the victim of a brutal rape forgive her rapist in order to heal? This idea is ludicrous to anyone who knows about processing trauma, yet a parallel form of this dynamic is exactly what average parents demand of average children in average families.

But are there cases in which it is psychologically appropriate for an adult child to excuse his parents for their errors? Many people, of course, could say, "But my parents were not brutal rapists. They were nice, loving people. Okay, maybe they didn't buy me the blue Mongoose bicycle I wanted for Christmas when I was twelve, but they didn't crush my soul."

"Or did they?" I ask.

The more I study perfectly normal people's childhoods the more I argue that they most certainly did crush your soul, that is, crush the essence of your self and your truth and your passion as a person. Most people block out their crushing history. They don't remember splitting off their terror at one, crying themselves to sleep at two, swallowing their rage at three, dousing the flames of their longing at four and quelling their rebellion at five. They have buried their pain and blotted out their memory. That makes it easy to trivialize the subject of forgiveness and to see the brutal rape analogy as something "out there" and "unrelated to me" and "not remotely analogous to my relationship with my parents."

I have an example from my own life. As a child I became an expert at forgiveness. No matter what my parents did to me, I was, to use their words, gifted at "turning the other cheek," "being the bigger person" and "being mature about things." I was even proud of myself for this. I felt I had incredible self-control. Yet it wasn't until I was well into my chronological adulthood that I discovered I had only mastered the art of selling myself out. I was an expert dissociator. Without a self to be connected to, I of course found it easy to forgive: after all, I felt none of the pain they inflicted on me. Yet in the shadows of my personality, hidden behind my poised façade and disconnected from my consciousness, there lived an abandoned, terrified little child, cowering in fear of more rejection. And he felt everything, but simply wasn't consciously aware of it.

Here I think of twenty-year-old Vanessa, a young woman I have known for years who recently had a major psychological breakdown. I remember her as a little girl: sparkling, emotionally connected and socially gifted. Then, when she was six, her hippie parents gave up their New York City apartment, uprooted her from her life and took her with them to Ecuador to live on a commune. This devastated her. When they returned to New York six years later she was broken. She had dissociated from her feelings and lost the passion in her eyes. She simmered with a repressed anger that occasionally surfaced in meanness and bullying toward littler children, which was a replication of what her parents had done to her. Just once she admitted to me how much she resented her parents for ripping her out of her life, and in that moment I felt the old fiery-eyed Vanessa.

But the rest of the time she said she forgave them. She couldn't tolerate breaking her dissociation and by her mid-teens she got high on marijuana every day (and not infrequently on painkillers) to keep her feelings at bay. But that didn't work and eventually her feelings found their way out through the lens of psychosis. At one point she beat up her mother, accusing her of stealing one of the hemispheres of her brain, which I considered a rather apt metaphor for her historical reality. Now I hear that Vanessa is back living with her parents and taking antipsychotics. She is a shell of what she once was and as a side effect of her pills has put on sixty pounds. Her parents, who live in their own cloud of dissociation, think her mental problems have been caused by her diet. But the sickest irony I heard, from a mutual acquaintance, is that "her parents have forgiven *her*."

This story is extreme but typical. They abused her, she dissociated from it and labeled it forgiveness because she needed her relationship with them, then she did drugs to shore up her dissociation. Eventually her wounded inner child, in a desperate attempt to save her soul, burst through her dissociation in a swell of madness and got *her* labeled as the problem— and got her placed on even heavier, more dangerous drugs to bury her feelings. Meanwhile, I don't mean to say it was right for her to beat up her mother, because I see that as an expression of unprocessed and acted out rage, but I do see her parents' crimes toward her as far more serious and devastating than anything she did to them.

As an alternate story, I will now let a friend of mine, Jonathan, speak for me. Jonathan is in his sixties. He spent decades out of contact with his parents because of their cruelty toward him when he was a child. He spent those decades studying himself, exploring the ways in which he replicated the unhealthy things they did to him and working to break his dissociation and to integrate his authentic self.

Recently Jonathan's father died and Jonathan returned home to the funeral. There he reconnected with his 93-year-old mother, whom he had long labeled "a barbarian" for her treatment of him. She had regularly psychologically and physically tormented him when he was little. Yet since the funeral he has been talking on the phone with her a couple of times a week, which he said, to his surprise, he mostly enjoys.

This confused me.

"Does this mean that you forgive your mother?" I asked, curious how he would respond.

"You know," he replied, "I hate the word 'forgiveness.' It's so misused in our culture and for that reason I don't really use it. When people say 'forgive' they really mean 'forget,' or even more so, 'deny.' I have not forgotten what she did to me and I don't deny how it wounded me. I know full well how cruel she was and how it warped my life."

"Yet you talk on the phone with her," I countered. "Often."

"Well," Jonathan said, "for years I didn't see her, and now that she's 93 I lost my fear that she could harm me. And I don't talk with her for her sake; I do it for *mine*. To be honest, I'm fascinated with her. For decades I avoided this barbarian, and now that I do speak with her I've come to realize how strong *I've* become. For so many years I was scared of her— thinking she could destroy me with one of her comments. But all that time

I was away from her I was growing — and she was growing weaker to me. Now she's harmless, just a little, lost old lady. And now that I find her harmless I can satisfy my curiosity about her. And I realize I have a lot. She's a person from a different world — and yet she was the most important person in my world during the most vulnerable years of my life. She grew up with an outhouse for a toilet and she had her Christmas presents delivered by horse sled. Her parents punished her by hitting her legs with a long willow switch. I also think she was molested, but she's never admitted it to me directly. But for all those years I was away I never got the chance to know the story of her childhood and to find out what created her character — and motivated her to treat me the way she did. So now I'm taking my opportunity."

"So you're not letting her off the hook for what she did."

"Oh no!" replied Jonathan. "Not at all. She passed all that damage on to me and she *is* accountable and *always will be*. I'm fascinated by the person who created me and raised me and hurt me so much. She's the primary material of my life."

"But to get back to the word 'forgiveness,'" I asked, "do you feel you forgive her?"

"No," he replied quietly, shaking his head. "No, I don't. I don't forgive her for what she did to me. And I don't forgive my father either. I don't see forgiveness as the point. That word has lost meaning to me."

Chapter 7: Romantic Relationships

Romantic relationships make an excellent place to reenact our unresolved childhood dynamics with our parents. Romance's combination of intimacy, intensity and vulnerability offers us a nearly perfect canvas onto which we can paint our conflicted childhood longings, resentments, struggles and forgotten memories. From what I have observed, one of the main factors motivating people to enter romantic relationships is parental rescue fantasy: the powerful unconscious hope that our parents, disguised as a romantic partner, will finally come back to save us from our childhood misery. That said, I do not wish to minimize the potential beauty of romance: the real nurturance, the underlying friendship, the genuine bonding and the healthy attraction; these can also exist. But to what degree is a romance healthy and to what degree is it imbued with parental rescue fantasy?

I believe the answer is surprisingly simple: the healthiness of a romantic relationship depends upon the degree to which we—that is, each of us and each of our partners—have broken away from the troubled sides of our parents. Where we have healed our childhood wounds and become emotionally independent adults we can experience the purity of real connection. Where we have not we will unconsciously be guided by neediness, not love.

Yet most people have little idea how damaged they are from childhood. They're largely blind to their inner world, puppets to it even. They don't know how to love themselves fully because their childhood wounds prevent it; instead they try to get their partners to do it for them. They want to find their perfect "other half" in someone else yet don't realize that that their missing perfection actually lives buried in their own unconscious. They have been deluded by the power of the drug of love.

Excavating our inner history is very painful because it requires that we feel the truth of our ancient trauma. This involves not only indicting our parents but indicting the sides of ourselves that are replicated versions of them. When relationships don't work out few people use this as an opportunity to study their own wounds. Most instead just see their partner's flaws. They say their partner "was a rotten person" or "was an infant masquerading as an adult" or "was selfish" or "was incapable of meeting my needs," as if that is a partner's job. It's not. But for many these beliefs provide justification enough for jumping back in the ring, ignoring their own inner world and immediately seeking out a new relationship. They delve back into dating and romance and sex—or, most tragically, into having children and thereby creating the best objects onto whom they can project their unresolved childhood feelings and patterns. After all, their young children can't divorce them; their partners can.

Staying out of relationships is too difficult for many people. It's going cold turkey off the drug. That causes an eruption of the unresolved childhood feelings of abandonment, rejection, loneliness and betrayal. This can be overwhelming, which is why so many people find themselves terrifyingly unwilling or unable to leave one romantic relationship until they have a new one, based on the same essential emotional dynamics, ready and waiting in the wings.

But many couples stay together for years, even for a lifetime, raising children and seeming so happy and healthy. Are they? From what I have observed most couples stay together for the comfort. They are like functional alcoholics, able to manage their dosage of the drug. They have perfected the art of burying most of their feelings, hopes, dreams and desires. They have become masters of compromise. They're not growing in anything near an optimal way, if at all. Instead they have largely died inside and they accept that. They do not work to break from the sick sides of their parents because this would upset their relational homeostasis. Although they may never make the tabloid magazines as steamy romantic ideals, they actually are quite the ideal in another sense; they have become normal.

But are those of us committed to breaking up with the sickness of our parents then relegated to a life of singleness and celibacy? I have been questioning that for years, exploring it deeply. And I wish to share the results of my explorations in light of the themes of this book. For ten years, essentially the whole of my thirties, I was celibate and almost entirely avoided following the lead of any romantic feelings I had for others. Instead I focused my energies, the energies many people put into romance, on healing myself. I studied my inner world, worked to unravel the knots of my traumas and continued to break away from my parents.

Life had taught me that if romance were ever to return to my life then healing my inner wounds would be the thing to make it possible.

But do I recommend this to others? Celibacy, especially for passionate people who retain a connection with their sexual feelings, is a tough road. Many people cannot handle it. It makes them too miserable; they need to jump back on the love drug. Others it causes to shut down and dissociate, which is why many celibate people are bland and out-of-touch. And it causes others to act out through other addictions or perverse forms of sexuality. It is difficult to manage the energy that celibacy calls forth from within. It's like being a sailboat in a very heavy wind. If you have the strength to hold fast you will be propelled forward into the waves. But if you lack the strength the wind will rip your sail or snap your mast.

Yet I do recommend that many people *try* celibacy—especially if they are open to the idea and feel they can use it for their own evolutionary betterment. Celibacy can help people attain more clarity about themselves as individuals, which is key to becoming independent from their parents— their actual parents and their mentally internalized parents. Celibacy gives us the opportunity to define our psychological and physical boundaries in the most precise of ways. It is also a chance for us to develop our relationships with ourselves, in a sense to return to the drawing board of our own conscious conception of our existence as individuals and redefine ourselves as human beings. Sometimes, in my experience, there is no better way than a period of celibacy for us to find out who we are.

Yet, for all the value I have gained through celibacy—and in many ways because of it—I am now exploring romance in a new way. In the last couple of years I have reentered the world of romantic relationships, albeit cautiously. When I was a teenager and in my twenties I threw caution to the wind and followed the lead of my parents and my culture. I jumped headlong into romance and sexual interaction, and despite whatever fun I had, frankly, I couldn't handle it emotionally. Mostly this was because I was replicating in my romances my relationships I had *with* my parents— yet I didn't even know that this was happening. It was unconscious, and, I now see, inevitable. I had too much unresolved material inside me to allow my relationships to be healthy yet, ironically, and in spite of that, I had too much healthiness inside me to let myself shut down and become compromised. So in that sense, I can now see that my path toward celibacy bore a certain inevitability. It was a logical, if temporary, outcome to my psychological trajectory. I needed it—and it helped me.

Now I am much more healthy, much more aware of myself and my actions. I have taken great strides in breaking up with my parents, both externally and internally, and this allows me a lot more psychological freedom to be healthier in romance—and actually in all areas of my life. I have also seen this pattern in others: the more people define their healthy individuality by breaking from their parents, the more they can live satisfying lives and have more satisfying relationships, be they romantic or not, with others. That said, in my case I know I am not fully healed, because I see and feel that some of the poison from my past still lives within me. I still have parental rescue fantasy, but a lot less than before.

All in all, this translates into me being much healthier in romantic relationships than I used to be. I see others more for who they are and less for whom I want them to be. And I love this, though I naturally still aspire to become healthier in my future.

The recent relationships I have had, minimal as they might be by conventional sex standards, tend to be much more healthy, boundaried, emotionally intimate and genuine—and fun—than ever before. They are also based much less than ever before in my life on the templates of my relationship with my parents. I find this invigorating. It helps that I am now much more patient and careful around expressions of sexuality. I prefer to court, not to jump into bed. Although I am by no means anti-sexuality—because I see our sexuality as a vital part of who we are—I have come to recognize how risky sexual interaction can be. It fertilizes parental rescue fantasy like nothing else. Sexual interaction can so easily turn a gentle, budding friendship with the potential for real goodness into a morass of confusion and pain and hurt feelings.

Yet I have learned all of this through exploration. And part of my exploratory process involves testing and making mistakes. I have made my fair share. I frankly don't know how to avoid them. For that reason I remain all for exploration, as long as it doesn't push the risk quotient too far. Yet how far is too far? I am not entirely sure. One thing I do know, though, is that sexual intercourse is very risky; aside from its emotional risks—and risks of disease transmission—look at all the children it has produced, and the aborted children too. For all of these reasons, I don't know if, or to what degree, I'll ever have sex again. At this point I actually feel like I've returned to being a virgin. Or as one young woman recently told me about herself, which I really respected, "After a few years of celibacy, my virginity grew back. I wasn't raised to treasure sex. I was raised to squander it. Now I'm learning to wait—and to love myself. It's been an adventure."

Yet I know many people who have done a lot of inner work who seem to be happy and stable in romantic relationships. Are they? On one level I believe they are. But on another level I am skeptical because I believe our disturbed world and our screwed-up childhoods have taught us so many wrong things about happiness. As regards these couples, is their happiness the comfort of dissociation or the deep pleasure of a connection with inner truth? Do they love each other as mature individuals or do they cling to each other unconsciously as semi-desperate children? From what I have observed, most people's happiness skews much more toward the dissociative pole, but even the more evolved people I know seem to live with a mix of the two. It isn't always easy to sort out the proportion, because the unhealthy so closely mimics the healthy. And even I, who consider myself pretty healthy, can become confused about this in myself, especially when romance is involved. Romantic feelings can so easily cloud the vision, because the parental rescue fantasy is so tantalizing.

Yet I let myself continue to explore. I learn from my romantic relationships. I learn from my partners and I hope they learn from me. But I also do my homework. I spend fifty or a hundred times more time with myself, in my own head and with my own feelings, interacting with myself in my journal or in some other form of my own private dialogue, than I do interacting romantically. My priority in life is to grow, that is, to continue to break from the sick sides of my parents and to become my own real, true self. If romance can nurture this side of me then I welcome it.

Yet my experience so far has shown me that so much of healing is a solitary process. We can be encouraged and motivated by others, but our primary relationship in life is with ourselves—our own true, golden inner self. And that is the basis for all other relationships. All relationships with others, including romantic relationships, stem from that marriage within. And although I am well aware that we are a social species and will always strive to connect as deeply with others as we are able, which I cherish, I still think some of this work, some profound part of it, has to be done outside of relationships with others, perhaps even far from it. And until we can do that, I really am not so sure we're ready to really enter deep, fully open, fully vulnerable and intimate relationships with others.

Chapter 8: Having Children

If it is hard to be in participant in a healthy romantic relationship, it is even harder to be a healthy parent. Having children is the absolute easiest way for us to act out, rather than work out, our unresolved childhood conflicts. The power differential between parent and dependent child is too great for us to avoid the temptation. Power corrupts and it corrupts parents first and foremost.

It might raise a few eyebrows that I include a chapter on having children in a book on breaking up with parents. The main eyebrow I raise for myself, which I will explore more thoroughly later in the chapter, is this: if I address this chapter, to one degree or other, to people who are parents or might aspire to become parents, am I not also simultaneously addressing the greater theme of this book to their future children? That is, would I be also encouraging your future children to someday break up with you?

My answer: in a way, yes. I encourage everyone to break up with the unhealthy sides of his parents. If I had children I know that the healthiest sides of me would only wish the same for them. They deserve it!

Meanwhile, my hope for parents or parents-to-be is that they do the breaking up with parental sickness themselves. The more they follow this path the less they place the burden for breaking up on their children. After all, someone has to break the vicious cycle. Why not do it sooner, generationally speaking, than later?

But this is theory—and one, again, that I will address more in the coming pages. What about practical reality? When are you or I ready to have children of our own?

This question is fairly easy for average people, because they don't think about it much. They haven't delved too deeply into what their parents did to them and as such don't know how much they missed in childhood and by extension how much their future children deserve. Instead they go the societally easy route, and don't admit to themselves that unconsciously this is their real reply: "I am ready to have children because I feel like it. Yes, it would be nice if I had more money or a better partner or a more relaxed job or more supportive friends or more free time, but I want kids and my situation is good enough. Therefore I'm ready."

This question becomes much more complicated for you who are breaking deeply with your parents, because by acknowledging that your parents were unable to live up to their responsibilities to you, you are likely to have a much greater ability to empathize with your historical child. And by extension you have more empathy for all children, that is, for their needs. As such, you recognize that what might seem to be "good enough" really is not good enough.

So by what criteria should you assess your own readiness to have a child, if you agree that readiness involves creating for the child the optimal trauma-preventing and growth-inducing context?

Here they are:

First, you need to fully resolve your own childhood traumas. By breaking from your parents and fully healing your historical wounds you unravel and ultimately dissolve the internalized parts of them that have become implanted in your head and lose your unconscious drive to take advantage of anyone, most especially your child. This is the way to break the intergenerational cycle of trauma, and also, at least in theory, to dissolve the future motivation for your child to want to break up with you.

Second, you need a fantastic partner, one who has met the previous criteria. Every child deserves a team of two parents fully resolved in their own childhood issues. With this partner of quality you have an equal to lean on, an equal to back you up and an equal to share this most precious mission of life.

Third, you need to have a lot of free time and energy and motivation and resources — and so does your partner. You both need enough youth, physical health, money and passion to make this possible. Your child deserves the best of your presence and the presence of your partner.

And finally, you need a mature, healed social milieu. No child deserves to be brought up in social isolation, even the social isolation of two healed parents. You need healthy, motivated, vibrant friends—friends who have also broken with the unhealthy sides of their parents—to help you out because they love you and love your child. You need a wealth of enriching activities to keep your child engaged. You need to live in a safe place, free from crime, poverty, war, unnecessary danger, cruel and average schools, other traumatized children and violence. And you need to live in a place that allows your child full access to free space, privacy, wilderness, animals, wildlife, art, natural food, physical activity, music, dancing, healthy companions, healthy friends, healthy guides who take the child's side and child's pace, countless fun things to do and a healthy community.

If it sounds like I am setting the bar insanely high, I would disagree. The bar I set for healthy and appropriate parenting is not insanely high, just impossibly high for anyone I have ever met. We are a species in a trance, lost and confused and clinging to denial as we destroy our children and destroy the delicate ecological balance of the planet that is their future. Our species is so sick that it tries to silence those who want to wake us up —first by silencing the cries of children and second by undermining those adults who hear these cries and know what they mean.

As such, I set the bar at a reasonable, logical and obvious level. What child deserves any less?

Yet people criticize me with the following: "But if everyone followed your advice no one would have kids and humans would go extinct!"

My reply is this: "Who *is* following my advice? Are you? And what, when we get down to brass tacks, *is* my advice? My real advice is that the most mature people put their energy into growing even more mature, breaking from their parents, becoming the best people they are capable of becoming and changing the world. And if enough of us work toward this goal, the world *will* change. Meanwhile, there are presently countless billions of wounded children walking this planet. It seems ludicrous for me that the healthiest people among us would want to increase that number." [11]

And others criticize by saying, "Parents don't need to be perfect to raise healthy children. In fact, if parents were perfect they'd make their children weak and narcissistic. Children grow strong in the face of adversity. In many cases trauma makes the world more beautiful, because it inspires creativity and motivation and beauty in some of our best artists and thinkers."

And I reply: "How crazy is that? These are the arguments of a denial-pusher. It is not trauma that makes us special, rather, it is our authentic self and the push of that authentic self to be real and to speak the truth at all cost. Trauma is what *limits* the beauty of the world and at best trauma

---

[11] I also explore this question of my broader point of view in the book's final chapter.

forces the authentic self to express itself through a tinier, more focused lens that sometimes gets titled 'artistic.' If trauma really begets beauty and creativity then the most traumatized areas of the world would be the most creative and beautiful. Are people in the densely populated city slums of India or sub-Saharan Africa the most creative? Were they in Stalinist Russia?"

The reality has been shown to me repeatedly by my life experience: children with the healthiest parents in the healthiest external contexts are the most alive. They are the happiest, learn the quickest, interact the most gently and empathically, have the most fun, make friends the most easily, have the broadest interests, are the least bored, watch the least television (at least in the developed world), spontaneously eat the healthiest, have the healthiest bodies, cry the least, sleep the best, trust the most easily, have the best instincts and love themselves the most. They are less interested in street drugs and are less likely to end up in the psychiatric system. They have the strongest senses of self. They know who they are and they know what they like — and know correctly that what they like is good for them. And as they grow older, they love others the most naturally. This is a logical consequence of what they experienced in their childhoods.

Children with healthier parents also have less reason to hate their parents, though ironically they sometimes hate their parents more overtly because they feel safer and more confident to do so. They simply have a stronger connection with their inner selves and can fight back against their traumatizers more comfortably. What I have observed is that many in the new generation of people who are realizing the truth of parental horror and who are breaking from their parents actually come from the upper echelons of the *least traumatized*. It is the easiest for them to realize what happened to them, the easiest for them to face their inner horrors and the easiest to break from their parents, because they have the most going for them. It is still hell for them to break away, because they have to go through the same quality of suffering that we all do, but they just have to go through less quantity.

Here I think of a new friend of mine, Karen, age 26. She summed this up best for me.

"I could never figure out," she said, "why I of all people hated my parents so much. Most of my friends got treated a lot worse by their parents than I did by mine yet they seemed to get along fine with them. Eventually I realized that that itself *was* the crux of it: the worse a parent is the more they break their kids' independent streak and make it harder for them to break away."

"But that's not always apparent on the surface," I pointed out, "because I know people who had it so rotten in childhood that they cut off their lousy parents pretty easily. For them it was like, 'Goodbye and good riddance.' But at the same time they carried all their parents' bad behavior along with them into all their new relationships."

"Yeah," added Karen, "it's like they *cut off* their parents—or maybe just cut off one parent—but didn't really *break away* from them. And from what I've seen, those people don't really fit in socially with healthier people who are breaking away at deeper levels."

"I think that's exactly it," I said. "They got screwed over by their parents yet haven't figured out how similar they actually *are* to their parents."

From this I take the step into deriving a simple take-home message to potential parents: If you want to be a good parent please heal your own wounds, heal all of them and be confident that you've done so before you seriously consider having children. The unresolved child within you is the real child you need to embrace and heal and raise. The degree to which you do not devote yourself first and foremost to the child within you is the degree to which you will fail your flesh-and-blood offspring, because you will pass on to him, by overt or subtle trauma, all the things you never faced in yourself. Thus, you will put him in the same dilemma that you are in now: whether to heal or to close his eyes and pass on these wounds to the next generation. Thus, if you have children and traumatize them even a little bit then I write this book not primarily for you but for your future children. If you traumatize your children even a little bit or if I traumatize mine they will have full right and responsibility to break from you and me and leave us in the dust.

And by the way, it's probably evident from my writing, but it's worth noting that I have no biological children. And I seriously doubt I ever will. My mission on this planet is different; I figured out long ago that procreation was contrary to my mission. In some ways this saddens me, because I think given different life circumstances I would have loved becoming a parent. I loved raising animals as a child and always assumed I would someday parent human children of my own. But life has taken me on a different course than I expected. Instead I work, and have long worked, to parent myself—and, through that, to create a different sort of living legacy. Take this book, for instance: in a sense it is one of my children. I have struggled to nurture its path toward independence.

Chapter 9: Siblings, Part 1

Many of us, when we were children, found our relationship with our siblings to be one of the easier places to replicate the best and the worst of our relationships with our parents. This is why some people absolutely love their siblings and others absolutely hate them. Most sibling relationships, however, replicate some combination of the good and the bad and thus progress into adulthood in some degree of conflict.

If you are breaking from your parents, ideally your siblings would walk the healing path alongside you and away from your parents. Although this sometimes happens, more often than not it does not, for two reasons: (1) when your siblings were young children they needed your parents much more than they needed you, and (2) most siblings haven't really grown much since then and thus have not shifted their loyalties. And the degree to which they have not shifted their loyalties is the degree to which they remain dangerous to you.

Here I think of a young woman I know, Stacey, whose younger brother Brad was in many ways her closest peer in childhood. Stacey long felt that Brad should be the most obvious ally for her life's journey. They sprang from the same womb and were only seventeen months apart in age. They had countless overlapping experiences, friendship circles and holiday memories. They shared years of the same childhood bedroom, the same favorite television shows, the same kids' books and also four grandparents. And for many years they were so close that they even knew what the other was thinking without saying it. However, when Stacey began breaking from their parents, she learned whose side Brad was primarily on: theirs. Brad largely blamed her for breaking away and tended to see her as a betrayer, yet couldn't see how both of them had been fundamentally betrayed by their parents. It was too painful for him.

A similar thing happened between another woman I know, Katie, and one of her stepbrothers, Jason, whose mother married Katie's father when Katie and Jason were early teenagers. From the beginning Jason and Katie were fast friends. They had a lot of fun times together and bonded over music, sports, mutual friends and love for the outdoors. Yet for years Katie's father was jealous of Jason and belittled him, and what Katie came to realize was that her father secretly wished Jason didn't exist, because he "stole" her father's new wife's attention. Begrudgingly, however, her father paid some attention to Jason and became a sort of father figure to him nonetheless.

Several years later when Katie began breaking away from her father, Jason took her father's side unconditionally. Jason said he wouldn't have contact with her unless she reconciled with her father. This was painful to her and put her in a position where she had to decide which relationship was more important to her: hers with Jason or hers with her own authentic self. She chose her authentic self. At that point Jason cut contact with her. Several years have now passed and Jason remains close to her father and close to the family system in general. He remains in denial of the deeper emotional content of his relationship with her father; it is simply too painful for him to consider, much less process. Katie, on the other hand, has a whole new circle of friends: "My family of choice," she calls them.

Yet I know others who compromise when facing this decision. I think of Tammy, whom I met while traveling, who broke contact with her parents in her early-twenties. By that point her father had remarried and had two new sons who were seven and eight years old. Her little half-brothers didn't understand why she no longer called or came by and sometimes they would telephone her and ask her to come over. She tried to explain to them why she didn't want contact with their father, but she had difficulty explaining her reasons because they were so young—and because she felt guilty for not maintaining contact with them. After a few years of staying away, she started coming over to her father's house for dinner occasionally, just to see the boys.

"How has that been?" I asked.

"You know," she replied, "mostly awful, aside from seeing my brothers. I detest seeing my father, and catching all the subtext in his words and behavior, and I feel emotionally hung over for days afterward. But I do love the boys. So I go. That's my compromise."

"But it sounds like you feel your compromise is worth it?"

"Yes," she replied. "For now, it is. But if I wasn't so close with my brothers I would never go around there. It's too toxic for me. Sometimes

I fantasize about adopting them and getting them out of there. The weird thing is that they don't even realize how toxic that home is. To them it's just normal. Then again, that's how I thought it was until I was a few years older."

Others, however, sacrifice their relationship with much younger siblings in order to break away. I think of a friend of mine named Gerald, whose mother had him when she was nineteen and subtly and sometimes not-so-subtly resented him throughout his childhood because she blamed him for denying her a proper young adulthood. When he turned twenty he broke away from her and from his father and moved to Alaska. His mother was only in her late-thirties by that point and had had twin daughters with his father only three years earlier. Gerald said that he loved his twin sisters but realized that he had to let go of his relationship with them in order to save himself.

"How did that feel?" I asked him.

"Crappy," he replied. "Really crappy. But I realized that if I'd stuck around my parents in order to have a relationship with the twins I'd just end up getting fucked up worse and wouldn't be of much use to them anyway. And, to be honest, I resented the very idea that I'd lost so many years of my childhood because of my screwed-up parents and now I was risking losing my young adult years because of my screwed-up parents' decision to have *more* kids. It's like, when was it *my* turn to be free? And I don't want to sound selfish, but the fact is, *I* didn't choose to create my twin sisters. I mean, if anyone had asked me my opinion I would have said my parents could have done the world a service by getting sterilized years ago. What scares me, though, is that my sisters are going to grow up on my parents' side, thinking I'm selfish and the family enemy, which is how my parents have recast me to everyone who will listen to them. That scares me. I hope someday the twins and I will be allies, but I am not counting on it. I've turned into a big, convenient, family scapegoat. That's a big part of why I got out. It was do or die for me."

I understand this all too well. In my own personal case, I find it dangerous to have intimacy with my siblings. And it's not only my siblings: I cannot, on an emotional level, safely be close with anyone who remains close with my parents. My parents, after all, tried to emotionally kill parts of me and still would if they could. And I remain partially vulnerable. So I protect myself. But, if my siblings *were* to leave my parents, if my siblings *were* to get real and get honest and side with their own authentic selves first, I would gladly have relationships with them again. In fact, I would crave it; who better to have as allies than one's healthy siblings? Who better to mirror the truth of one's childhood than those who were there as peers, peers who lived behind the closed doors of the family façade? But in the meantime my siblings simply are not allies—not to my authentic self.

Here I think of an acquaintance, Scott, age 32, who learned this the hard way after not speaking with his parents or siblings for four years. Recently his younger brother called him, out of the blue, saying he "just wanted to catch up." They talked for an hour and shared about all sorts of personal things, which thrilled Scott.

"I never thought of my brother as such a good listener," Scott told me. "He was really curious about my life and my thoughts and my reasons for having done what I did. He listened so well—and he seemed to care. He even said he missed me and respected me. Because of that I got hopeful and even excited that maybe he, *someone* in the family, was really considering doing what I was doing—getting away from our family and starting an honest life. I mean, he wasn't saying he exactly wanted to, but he really was taking it all in."

"Wow," I said. "I wouldn't have expected that."

"Well," said Scott, "don't hold your breath. It wasn't until a few weeks later that I found out my brother had taken everything I shared with him back to my family and spread it all around for them to feed on. It was like he won the contest of who could get the most information out of me. And here I thought we were building something new. I felt like a total fool— and I was also ticked off. And I also realized how little my brother had changed. Back when we were kids he used to do the same thing: to take anything private that he knew about me and bring it to my parents to get them to love him more. And what's really pathetic is that my sister and I used to do that too toward him and toward each other. We all did it. That's the only way we got love. My parents were masters of divide and conquer: that was their strategy for raising us. We were always at each other's throats, looking for vulnerabilities, exploiting weaknesses, taking advantage of our shaky alliances."

"Did you confront your brother for betraying you?" I asked.

"Sort of," replied Scott with a sad smile. "I sent him an email after I figured out what he did, thanking him in a tongue-and-cheek way for 'respecting the privacy' of our conversation."

"Did he reply?"

"Yes," he said. "Actually he did. And it was interesting: he dropped the pretense of being nice and he said that I needed to 'grow up' and to not try to 'create private factions in the family.' He really said that! Truth is, he didn't empathize one bit with what I shared with him in our hourlong conversation. But I think secretly he felt ashamed for what he did. But he'd never admit it."

"Did you reply to him after that?" I asked.

"No," he said. "I didn't see the point. Despite whatever he might feel deep in his heart, he's on their side. And what's pathetic is that deep down in my heart I knew it the whole time I was talking on the phone with him. I wanted to *believe* he'd changed. I guess I always wanted an ally in the family. We had been close in some ways when we were kids, playing basketball and fishing and all that, even sometimes talking about girls and life and stuff. It's painful to realize that at least for now it's over. It's dead. I can't go back to him because he'd just betray me again. I guess I have to relearn the lesson every few years. After all, it's not the first time I've opened up emotionally with naïve hope and then gotten a wake-up kick in the rear end."

"Hmm," I replied. "I hear you."

For some people, though, breaking with their siblings is easier than breaking with their parents. Some people consider their siblings to be even more hurtful than their parents were. Recently someone who saw one of my internet videos on parental trauma commented that his siblings committed "99 percent of the abuse" against him and that his parents were much less to blame. Although I don't doubt that his siblings behaved abusively toward him, I cannot imagine how his parents bore so little responsibility. From what I have observed, behind every abusive sibling is an abusive parent. Siblings, at their worst, are agents of the parents. After all, lovely, loving, wonderful, caring, respectful, responsible parents do not create children who abuse each other. Abusive children are the byproducts of abusive parents. Children are born perfect and only replicate onto others that which was done to them.

Yet in so many families and within the minds of so many individuals this knowledge is taboo. Many parents even secretly delight that one of their children is overtly abusive to his siblings, because his abuse takes the focus off *their* abusiveness and sometimes off a subset of their abusiveness: their neglect. In these cases they can then blame any problem in the family on him, this "abusive child." Over the years I heard several therapy clients initially describe having had decent, good-hearted parents and a rotten older brother or older sister: "the cause of all my family's problems."

I heard things like: "He destroyed us." "She ruined my parents' relationship." "He ruined my life." "She was evil." "He was a selfish monster." "She was a bad seed."

Rarely was the question asked by them about why their parents were so weak and incompetent to let this "bad seed" gain so much power in the family, much less why no one was able to intervene. Yet what I found most interesting is that few of these people, up until therapy (and some right through it), put much energy into exploring the situation's etiology, that is, into exploring what in the world caused this sibling to become "so evil." Believing in the myth of a "born-evil" sibling allows parental idealization to stay firmly in place. And parental idealization can be a real comfort drug.

Of course, one could say that perhaps it wasn't the parents who treated an abusive sibling in an evil way. Perhaps his abuse came from outside the family. Although that is theoretically possible, in my experience it isn't the case. Yes, of course non-family members, and thus non-parents, can and do abuse children and no one denies that. Extreme cases of this get major media attention almost every day. But non-familial abuse of children, especially young children whose very personalities are being formed, is a lot less common and far less significant than that which happens inside families every day. A child's first society and culture is his family system.[12] They have full access to his forming personality and they mold it. If it gets warped, it was primarily they who warped it.

And even if an outsider *does* get access to a child and abuses him, often the parents bear a great deal of responsibility for this. All too often they either neglected the child, such that outsiders gained access to him or such that he was drawn to outsiders for the parental-like love that he wasn't getting in the home. Or perhaps his parents abused him more covertly and his more overt abuse by outsiders was just a replication of that which he'd already received in the home. And sometimes parents even unconsciously let outsiders abuse their children in order to replicate the abuse that happened to the parents themselves from when they were children. I myself was abused by a nanny when I was a child. My parents didn't find out about it until quite a bit later. Yet it was they who put me into her hands, and according to them they never picked up the signs that she was abusive. Or maybe they quite clearly picked up the signs consciously or unconsciously, and put me into hands *because* of her abusiveness. Although not commonly spoken about because it violates the supposed sanctity of parental love, this is not an uncommon occurrence.

---

[12] Here, of course, I am speaking more about modern, Western cultures that have more discrete family units. But even in the non-Western cultures I have personally experienced and studied, the family system, however it is arranged, is the primary root of a child's existence. I am aware, though, that other cultures have some profoundly different family arrangements than those I have personally observed.

Meanwhile, for many people, blaming abusive siblings is a convenient way to let abusive parents off the hook for their crimes. How much easier and more comfortable to believe that a less important, secondary figure in your life failed you than to realize that the people who created your existence, your life's first and most basic and primal models of love, let you down. Grieving the failure of a sibling can hurt; grieving the failure of a parent is the most painful work of a lifetime.

Chapter 10: Siblings, Part 2

I have heard other permutations of people's relationships with their siblings that I find worth discussing. I have one friend, Donald, age 34, who cut all contact with his parents in his twenties because they were so virulently opposed to him being gay. His father mocked his sexual orientation and his mother wanted him to join the Marines and fight in Afghanistan "to make him a man." Yet Donald's brother, Keith, who was a year younger and straight, had always respected Donald. Keith was the first person Donald came out to and the two maintained a relationship. Yet Keith remained close to their parents. Although this disappointed Donald, he felt it worthwhile to maintain his relationship with his brother.

"You know," Donald said, "I love Keith. I really do. I mean, I see his limitations, because our parents are brutes and in some ways he's like them, but at the same time he helped save my life. He was always there for me in some basic way—not fully, but in some important way. And I can't forget that."

"How close are you now?" I asked.

"Well, we used to be closer," Donald replied. "I mean, Keith lives in our old hometown and he goes to the country club with my dad. He's not on my wavelength at all. But I know he admires me for standing up to them and breaking away and in his own way he lets me know this when he comes to visit. But he couldn't *really* handle being close friends with me.

He likes to talk to me about once a month and I know that whenever he has real problems he comes to me for discussion and support and doesn't go to them. It's like I give him energy from the outside world, mature energy. But mostly he's living in the family world. That's his real allegiance."

"Do you resent him?" I asked.

"Well, let's just say that I *used* to," Donald said. "Now I think I've accepted him for who he is. I used to hope he would move to the big city like me and leave our family behind and really give himself a chance for something new. But that wasn't him. Somehow he's like a kid: emotionally latched on to them. And I realized I couldn't change that. That's who he is. And the truth is, I think I can accept him for who he is. He doesn't badmouth me to our parents and he doesn't ask me too much about the deeper stuff. And somehow he doesn't bother me too much. And in a strange way he's really there for our parents, now that they're getting older and frailer, and that lets me off the hook from feeling guilty, because I'm not there for them at all."

"But they weren't there for you either," I said.

"No, they were not," said Donald, "but that's not how *they* see it. They see it that they were *totally* there for me, that they were *great* parents and that I'm a freak of nature whom they tried, unsuccessfully, to correct."

"Sick, eh?"

"Yeah," said Donald. "Sick. It's the story of my childhood. There's a reason I got the hell out of Dodge."

"Hmm," I said. "Makes sense."

"But at the same time," he added wistfully, "I really do wonder if I'm making some deep emotional sacrifices by staying close to my brother. I mean, I sometimes wonder if having any connection with him at all keeps me somehow close to them, like he's some sort of channel for my hope that someday they'll come back and love me properly. I do sometimes daydream about cutting him off like I've done with them—just moving on and declaring my family dead and really becoming my own totally new person—true to myself and true to life. But I'm not there yet. Yes, I'd probably do it if he did something to hurt me, but mostly I see him as a weak, broken guy who's basically pretty nice to me. So I keep him in my life—in a distant, mostly pleasant sort of way. It's really not that much of a sacrifice."

Now I think of Mike, a friend in his fifties, and who, for the first time in his life, is close with his sister.

"Valerie and I never had anything to do with each other," he said. "I didn't ever like her and she didn't ever like me. To me she was 'The Bitch' and to her I was 'The Little Bastard.' That's just how it was.

Basically, our parents turned us against each other as kids and that dynamic lasted for half a century. It's only changed in the last few years."

"Why?" I asked, with genuine curiosity.

"It's really weird," replied Mike. "A few summers ago we both started talking about our childhoods—on the telephone, from a thousand miles away—and we compared notes and realized that we'd both gotten a raw fucking deal from our parents: *the exact same raw fucking deal.* Without either of us knowing it we'd both been in therapy for our fucked up lives and we both realized we'd been separately talking with shrinks about the same shit. She went into couples counseling while she was divorcing her abusive shit husband and I'd been doing therapy because of my daughter committing suicide. And then, *bang,* one day we started talking about it—and it all came tumbling out. We'd both been abused by them and in the same basic way. Beaten, put down, deprived, whipped on the ass, the whole nine yards. And we were both angry as fuck. And our anger actually gave us a lot of strength to talk about it with each other and I started realizing, for the first time in my life, that dammit...I really loved her. And she loved me too! It was kind of amazing, because I never thought that any love at all could come out of our fucked-up redneck family."

"So you're friends now?" I asked.

"Yeah," he replied, wiping some tears from his eyes. "Yeah. I would never have believed I'd say that. But yes, that's what we are. We're friends. Buddies even. And our parents know this and it freaks them out. Valerie and I—'The Bitch' and 'The Little Bastard'—both stick it to them all the time. I'll tell my mom and dad, 'I just had a nice talk with Valerie on the phone.' And they'll get all nervous and be like, 'What did you guys talk about?' And I never tell them. Not a damn word. They can go fuck off."

"So they're scared of you being allies," I said.

"Hell yeah!" he replied. "They used to love it that we hated each other. Well, no more. Now we're a united front. And our parents can't do jack-shit about it. Sometimes I don't talk to my parents for six months or a year at a time and Valerie supports me. And if she wants to get away from them, well, I support her too. She's my touchstone—and never in a million years would I have predicted that I'd be saying that. I guess we just both grew up and faced reality a bit more. Life kicked us both pretty hard in the ass, but at least a bit of good stuff is coming out of it."

To study this from another angle, I know a different scenario in which two siblings are both simultaneously breaking from their parents. Although they would seem to have everything in common, in reality their relationship is fraught with friction. Rebecca, age thirty, whom I met through my website, has a sister, Jenna, who is two years her senior. Both somewhat independently came to the realization that their parents treated them destructively and both started breaking away. For a time Rebecca and Jenna grew quite close and supported each other emotionally, even living together and going to therapy together for a year. However, things changed when Rebecca started to recall events in their childhood in which Jenna had treated her cruelly and broken her down psychologically.

"Once those old feelings started coming up," Rebecca said, "I didn't feel so close to Jenna. I mean, I know that we were just kids back then and that she was miserable and acting out on me what our parents did to her, but still, *she* did those things to me. And I don't feel comfortable around her now, not in the same way."

"Do you still live with Jenna?" I asked.

"No," replied Rebecca. "I actually moved out. I had to. It was like, by being around her so much I couldn't feel the feelings I needed to feel in order to continue healing. I had to stuff my feelings that related to her and that made me resent her, which caused me to be rude to her. And then she'd feel hurt and lash out back at me. It was like childhood all over again. It was awful."

"Did you ever tell Jenna what was going on for you?"

"I did," she said. "In therapy. It was easier to have a sort of 'objective' referee there. The problem was, our therapist wasn't so objective and actually started taking Jenna's side. He felt I was acting out and didn't really get it. I mean, he didn't get the context and history of where my feelings were coming from. He was just all stuck in the 'here-and-now' and wasn't strongly enough on the side of my wounded child. So I quit the therapy and moved out."

"Has your relationship with Jenna changed since then?" I asked.

"Funnily enough," replied Rebecca, "it's actually gotten quite a bit better. I mean, I can be pissed at her in private for stuff she did twenty years ago. I can be as pissed as I need to be and as hurt as I need to be and I don't need to tiptoe around her bedroom in the apartment and hold a grudge when she takes too long in the shower and doesn't clean the mirror after brushing her teeth. It's really much better that we live apart. That was a setup for recreating our childhood dynamics and it was bringing me down. Now we see each other once every couple of weeks. And while it's not always easy for me, because I still have feelings that can swing into the negative, it's okay. Basically she's an ally for me. But I process our present relationship and our historical relationship in private—without her. Which is what I need. Privacy. Away from my biological family."

"And how is your relationship with her, from *her* perspective?"

"That's interesting," she replied. "Jenna's hurt that I don't want to be closer with her—and she really does try to acknowledge how she hurt me when we were kids. The thing is, she doesn't feel any resentment toward me from when we were little, because she doesn't feel I abused her at all.

So it's all easier for her. She'd hang out with me all the time if I'd do it. But I'm the one with the hurt feelings, so I need to be the one with better boundaries. And basically she respects that. She really works to respect my process."

"So she tries to acknowledge having abused you when you were little?"

"Yes," said Rebecca, "she does. And she does it pretty well. And that really helps. I actually respect her for it. And let's face it, if she didn't own what she did I don't think I could be close with her at all. But she knows she did some messed-up things to me and had a pattern of violating me. And she knows pretty much why she did it. So at least she's on my side there—and pretty much on the side of reality. But actually, when I'm really honest with how I feel, and this isn't easy to admit, I think she *does* hold some resentment toward me, deep down."

"How so?" I asked.

"For the fact that I was *born*. After all, Jenna was just two when I came along and because of that my mom basically abandoned her when I was a baby. Jenna got sent to daycare all the time and then off to Kindergarten. And basically it was because of my arrival on the scene. When we were kids our mother even told 'funny' stories—which weren't actually funny at all—about how much my sister resented my existence back then. I tried bringing this up with Jenna recently."

"And how did she take it?"

Rebecca shook her head: "She said she doesn't have any memory of resenting me. She really doesn't. She said it's also possible that our mother is lying about her resenting me. Our mother does lie a lot."

"Complicated stuff!" I said.

"You're telling me!" she replied. "But I still think that my mother is right here: that Jenna did resent me. I think my mother knows it, because it's true. It's just too logical not to be true. My mother had to reject Jenna to some degree when I was born. I've been around babies and little kids enough to know how much energy a baby demands from a parent and how much older siblings get the shaft when a new little baby comes along."

"Yes," I replied. "Sadly, that is pretty much the reality."

Shifting gears, I think of the story of Leo, a 43-year-old friend of mine who has a complicated sibling history with his younger brother Dale, who is a year younger. Leo told me that although in some ways he loved and protected Dale when they were children, he has distinct memories of abusing Dale too.

"I punched him occasionally and teased him a lot," he said, "and one time I even tried to get sexual with him—but at least I stopped when he was clearly not into it. Thank God for that. The older boys at school were sometimes trying to do sexual things to the younger or weaker boys—they did stuff to me—and I tried some of that with Dale. Doesn't feel good to say that, but it's the truth."

"That's courageous of you to admit," I said. "Most people never admit anything close to that."

"Well," replied Leo, "I realized that my salvation came from opening up and telling the truth. My quest has been to open up and be real. Frankly it's saved my life."

"How does your brother Dale take it that you are so open now?" I asked.

"Well," he replied, "Dale's a mixed bag. In some ways he respects my openness and in some ways it scares the living daylights out of him. He's pretty shut down in terms of talking about things. Yet he wasn't so perfect himself when he was younger. Although he definitely loved me in some ways, he also treated me pretty shitty at times. He used to psychologically rip me apart, really break me down, for some of my social weaknesses. It really messed with my head. When I think about it in perspective, our relationship was always mixed up, from the beginning. We were two neglected, abused kids acting out all our shit on each other, because in many ways we were all the two of us had. But in spite of the reality of it, for years I denied all the hurtful things I'd done to Dale, literally blocking them from my conscious mind because they were too painful for me to acknowledge. That is how dissociated I was back then."

"When did you start waking up?" I asked.

"In my twenties," Leo replied. "Somehow I started becoming aware of my traumas—the stuff my parents did to me, and didn't do *for* me. And there was a lot of stuff. It was then that I started speaking into a tape recorder, furiously actually, about the sick things I'd done to Dale—and to others, and to myself. And I feel comfortable saying 'sick,' and felt it even then, because I really felt sickened by a lot of the things I'd done. Basically, although I was always a good person at heart, I could see, with a few years of hindsight, that I'd also been a pretty wounded kid. And taking responsibility for those confused things I did really pushed forward my process of splitting away from my parents, because at some level I could just feel, without really even intellectually understanding where my feelings were coming from, that a lot of the rotten and twisted things I did to others came directly from them. Although I do blame the boys at school for some of the sexual stuff, I blame my parents even more for setting me up to be a victim of that. Coming out of my household, I had no idea how to have boundaries or strength in that area. My dad was a porn addict and my mom let him, and even indulged him in that—and it wasn't very hidden from me. By the time I was twelve I knew what they were up to. And not just that, but my self-esteem was shit because of how they treated me. So later, when I was in my twenties and I started waking up to reality, it was like I had a little bird of intuition that sang the truth into my ear—or into my heart and into my stomach is probably more accurate. At first I only felt it emotionally. The intellectual part came later, gradually, as I took more distance from them and gained the perspective to be able to put the pieces into some coherent mental order."

"How did this affect your relationship with Dale?" I asked. "I'm curious about that because I have siblings too, and haven't always been a great brother myself—far from it, in fact. I would imagine it must have been pretty profound for Dale to watch you go through all this, after all."

"It was," replied Leo. "It was a pretty damn intense time in both of our lives. I remember when I was in my mid-twenties and still had a fairly close relationship with him that I began openly taking responsibility for what I'd done to him. I told him pretty much all of the bad things I'd done that involved him, why I felt it was wrong—and some of it was blatantly wrong—and why I was sorry. Some of the stuff he knew, some he didn't."

"Damn," I replied. "Heavy stuff."

"Yeah," he said. "It was heavy. It actually messed up our relationship pretty badly, because in my family no one as far as I know had ever admitted any bad shit, except perhaps for ten or fifteen seconds in a moment of guilt or desire for pity—often a drunken moment—which of course never came attached to any sincere effort to change their sick behavior. I threw off the historical balance of things in a pretty hardcore way and Dale didn't know how to handle it. At first he followed my lead and admitted some things himself, which was kind of a revelation to me, to be honest, but eventually he pulled back—and then way, way back—

and took a different path. He actually kind of wigged out, to be fair. Ended up on antidepressants and all that shit. It wasn't pretty for a while there. And then when he got off the pills he turned all furious and full of rage and hysteria, which I couldn't quite hold against him, but then he just ended up blaming me as the 'sick one' in our family—as if I was the only 'sicko' in the whole family tree—and he let our hypothetically 'good' parents off the hook. Yet what was weird was that at the same time he was hating on me he wanted to maintain a relationship with me, that is, with the *old* me, the old, troubled, unconscious, in-denial, acting-out Leo who saw nothing, processed nothing, understood nothing and said nothing. That version of me was safer to our sick family, and certainly safer for Dale. The problem was, the old Leo was shriveling up and disappearing, and the new Leo was bursting through my personality. And though growing out of the old Leo pleased me, because it was saving my life and giving me hope, by and large it didn't seem to please my brother. He acted as if I were abandoning him and abandoning our parents, and from his actions he often seemed to hate me for it."

"That must have been confusing," I said.

"Tell me about it. At the time—that was twenty years ago, and went on for a few years—that stuff confused the shit out of me. Some days I regretted having told him so much about the foul things I did, because he seemed to lack any ability or desire to see my flaws in a broader context of anything."

"You mean like in the broader context of the deeper ills of your family?

"Exactly. Dale just didn't seem to want to study that. He wanted to see, or believe, that my actions had all happened in isolation, and therefore I, and I alone, random dumb-ass kid that I was, was solely to blame."

"Denial is a profound thing."

"You're telling me! It was sure convenient for him. So anyway, some days I regretted ever opening my mouth, and other days I felt overwhelmed and wondered if I might lose my own mind because of my feelings. I could barely function. My pain, my shame, my guilt—they knocked me for a loop and spun me around in circles. I could barely get out of bed. Yet I also fought for myself and continued to grow. I feel very lucky."

"And how's your relationship with Dale now?" I asked.

"Well," he replied. "I can't say it's great. It's not awful though. It's mostly peaceful. Over the years I have tried a few times to discuss with him, as rationally as I could, some of my observations about our family, but it didn't go anywhere. Dale does not want to know—he's made that clear. And in a sense, I think I understand: it's too painful. I think somehow, because of what my parents did to him—and they really did a lot worse stuff to him than I ever did, though I didn't help the situation, of course—he's more hurt than I am. More fundamentally damaged. And just not as committed to healing. Not as passionate, for some reason. And maybe somehow these things are connected — the fundamental damage and the passionate commitment to healing. I don't know. But anyway, I did learn, over time, and still am learning, that the truth of our childhood was not and is not too painful for me to know; I have to know, at whatever the cost. Some little light just shines in my head, or maybe in my heart, and I can't stop walking forward."

"It's actually cool to hear this," I stated. "Somehow it gives me courage."

"Thanks," he said. "And thanks for listening. But anyway, just to finish. So, what I've learned is that two very positive things came out of me taking responsibility for my sick behavior. The first is that I regained my self-respect. I now have nothing to hide. My cards are out on the table and I don't have to live in secrets or defend my confused past with denials, and I was the king of denial. The way I am now feels good. I know that part of me was an abuser and I know *why* part of me was an abuser. I know that in many ways I was a lousy brother, and I don't deny that and I never will deny it. And while it breaks my heart, I know that I never wished to be that way and that I am, day by day, becoming a better human being because of my *lack* of denial. I'm not that sick kid I used to be. And that feels great."

"And the second thing?" I asked.

"So the second positive thing comes out of the first. By opening up and being honest I've allowed myself to continue growing. I stopped playing the regular family game of seeing myself as perfect and everyone else as screwed up. Instead I was able to look at myself as a wounded, partially dissociated, partially self-rejecting person. This opened the door to my deeper feelings and to the pathway toward integration, so even if I have, for now, lost a brother—a real heart-to-heart brother that I used to wish Dale would become—I have gained a deeper brother in myself. To me that's a blessing. I hate to use those religious words, but sometimes I just can't help myself. It's a real, true blessing in this life."

SECTION 2: ACTION

Chapter 11: Journaling, Part 1

Breaking away from one's parents requires action. This action is a self-therapeutic process—a process of gaining knowledge and then moving forward based on the clarity that that knowledge provides. The basic essence of self-therapy is self-reflection: looking within and getting to know ourselves at all levels of our beings, flaws and all. For most of us this takes practice, because we were not raised to study ourselves and especially not to study the sides of ourselves and our families that our parents swept under the carpet.

People practice self-therapy in all sorts of ways. Some practice dream analysis, some practice meditation, some develop discussion-oriented friendships, some engage in formal healing-oriented study groups, some practice mind-body forms of focusing, some change their lifestyle, some practice inner dialoguing, some people draw and paint, some read psychology, some practice gentle exercise, some practice celibacy, some go to actual psychotherapy and some do combinations of many of these. And some people try different ideas of their own design. After all, we are each by nature unique and creative. Why not utilize our unique creativity to the fullest?

My most basic mode of self-reflection has been journaling and I credit it with helping to save my life. For that reason I wish to devote two chapters to it. I have been journaling since I was a teenager, long before I'd ever heard of self-therapy. For a few years I wrote solely by hand in a notebook and then I transitioned to typing my words into the computer, not only because I could type much faster than handwrite but because I liked to search old journal entries for keywords, key dates and key phrases —and searching handwritten notebooks proved unwieldy.

I still remember my first journal entries, when I was seventeen and so lost and alone in my family. Writing in my big, black notebook was, because I can think of no better word to describe it, *wild*. There I entered a forbidden and emotionally-charged world where for the first time in my life I had a special friend who loved me and listened to me and kept my confidences and didn't misjudge me. He let me express my feelings and explore why I was feeling them. He let me explore my relationships, my history, my hopes, my dreams, my desires, my weaknesses and my fears. He didn't gossip about me or pry into my sexuality like my mother did, he didn't resent me and bully me like my father did and he didn't humiliate me and emasculate me like some of my other relatives did. He just held on to my words, heard them silently and waited patiently until I was ready to return to him. Sometimes he waited weeks and sometimes he waited months. And I valued his patience.

My journal was precious to me and I guarded him carefully, drilling a hole through his pages and putting a padlock on him so that no one else would use his secrets against me. Locking him was a wise move in my family. My family had shaky ethics when it came to violating my psyche and comfortably defended their actions. And what is sad—which for years I could only admit to my journal, because I had no one else to share it with

—is that back then I was not so different from them. I tried to read other family members' journals as well. I was very much a part of my troubled family system.

Yet even with the lock, journaling was not easy for me. You'd think it would have been, considering the relief and refreshing pleasure it brought me. But things were not so simple and are not for many others I have witnessed. Journaling has its difficult sides, especially for people who get really honest on paper. Although I often suggested to people that journaling might benefit them, not many I've seen have taken up the practice, at least initially. Many I've spoken with have tried it only a few times and shared that it made them feel uncomfortable or self-conscious or confused or even overwhelmed.

I heard some people say things like, "I feel like I'm just writing a lot of nonsense when I journal. And I don't even feel like it's me who's writing it. What up with that?"

My hypothetical reply, based on my own personal experience: "Your authentic self is writing in your journal, but you're normally so distanced from your authentic self that it doesn't even feel like *you*. It takes time to become accustomed to your authentic self, because in your childhood family your authentic self was an alien being."

Or perhaps someone else asked me: "I thought journaling was supposed to make me feel good? Instead I get so emotional when I journal, sad or enraged, mostly, that I can't sleep afterward."

My hypothetical reply: "Journaling accesses the deeper feelings that you've buried. It's like opening up an infection and letting the air in—and the decay out. This is healthy, but it's important to journal wisely and in moderation. Healing takes time. It's like distance running: you don't just become good at it overnight. Also, maybe it's better to journal in the morning, so you have the whole day to process it. And maybe it's better to only journal once a week or so, maybe even less—or to have someone safe to process your journal entries with afterward, so you're not so alone with your feelings."

And someone else might have said: "I feel like someone's watching me when I journal, like looking over my shoulder and telling me that I'm a fool for writing down these personal thoughts."

My hypothetical reply: "My sense is that someone *is* watching you when you journal. It's the self-hating voices and thoughts implanted in you by your parents. They don't like what you're doing. When you journal you're engaging in guerrilla warfare against them and their embedded emissaries in your head. And that's against the rules. But you're *not* a fool to journal. There's nothing foolish at all about struggling to liberate yourself."

Or another person: "If I keep journaling like this I'm not ever going to want to speak with my parents again. And I can't afford that. I love them too much. I don't want to hate them."

My hypothetical reply: "You may actually be right about journaling killing your present relationship with your parents. But if telling the truth makes you hate them, it's probably worth considering why you love them so much."

Or another: "I feel like I'm weak because I can only bear to write a paragraph or two at a time. And then after I write I just have to go take a nap because I'm so exhausted. Is there something wrong with me?"

My hypothetical reply: "No, this sounds fine to me. It's about quality, not quantity. Maybe you said exactly what you needed to say right now. Also, for some people it takes time to build up your inner endurance. The part of us that tells the truth, that is able to speak the truth, is a muscle. And that muscle tends to atrophy within the family system. That's my own experience as well as that of many people I have talked with. For me, even a few years into journaling I often found it a labor to write out a few hundred authentic words at a time."

But I do not mean to imply that journaling is necessarily a foolproof method for connecting with the authentic self. I have known some people who journal regularly but cannot seem to get honest with themselves on paper. Instead they use journaling to shore up the wounded sides of themselves, to bolster their denial and to convince themselves that their unhealthy path is the right way. They defend their acting out as maturity and they repel thoughts to the contrary.

Here I think of an acquaintance, Kim, a 45-year-old woman who shared her journals with me. When I flipped through the handwritten pages, year after year, I saw an odd pattern: each individual journal entry, in which she wrote about her present-day interactions, started in one handwriting style and gradually morphed into an unrecognizably different one. The initial style was large, inconsistent and seemed hugely emotional. She wrote with pain, rage, fury and a good dousing of blame. According to her, everyone aside from herself she wrote about, such as her boyfriend, her boss, her friends, even her daughter, had somehow victimized her. She took no responsibility for anything, not even for having repeatedly and voluntarily participated in unhealthy interactions. Then, once she'd doled out the blame and convinced herself that she was right and they were wrong, her words calmed down, her style relaxed and her handwriting font shrunk and become more readable and more consistent.

But I saw evidence of neither self-reflection nor self-development in her writing.

"I write to relax myself," said Kim. "It makes me feel good. It soothes me."

"Do you ever sit down to write when you're not really upset or angry?" I asked. "I mean, do you ever write just to explore?"

She looked at my quizzically.

"No," she replied. "Why would I do that? Journaling for me is like taking a valium. And why would I take a valium if I was already feeling calm?"

In a way I could relate to her. I have done some of this myself, more commonly when I feel really angry or hurt. I have the old journal entries to prove it and I find these entries a valuable study of my own psychology. But my most productive journaling tends to happen when I am feeling calm enough to stay centered in my true self. There I use my analytical skills to help frame my emotional expression—to process and learn from it. It's a multifaceted process—a full inner workout, so to speak.

But I do not demand perfection from myself in my journal writing or anywhere in my self-therapy. Instead I settle for being as honest as I can in any given moment. Sometimes I may speculate incorrectly on things, sometimes I misread people and their motives, sometimes I am too harsh on myself (or others), sometimes I go off on wild-goose-chasing tangents and sometimes I have weird theories that do not later prove to hold water. And mostly I love myself enough to keep on walking forward regardless. This is how I grow.

Yet it took me a long time to accept this in myself. Coming from my critical family I didn't have a lot of leeway to be wrong about much. Being wrong meant that I was vulnerable to attack, so I, like Kim, clung desperately to being right. I was not conscious of being terrified that my façade would implode if I admitted errors or frailties, so I rarely admitted any, except silently and privately in my own self-reflective process. For a long time I was even too scared to admit many of my flaws to my journal; somehow I felt safer if they stayed hidden in my own head— semiconscious, dormant and unexpressed. It took a lot of time for me to admit more of my weaknesses. And I'm still improving at this.

What I have observed is that the degree to which people have terror of revealing their inner worlds, even to themselves in a journal, correlates to the degree to which their parents crushed their authenticity. The more healed or initially healthy they are the easier it is for them to open up spontaneously and be honest about whatever's going on inside.

Here I think of Terry, age 53, a marine biologist and part-time musician whom I bonded with over love of American country blues.

"It took me a long time to grow up enough to be honest with myself in my journal. For years I danced around the truth in my writing because I couldn't handle it. But in the last ten years, since my parents died, my journaling has really flowered. It was like I became free to be honest. Really honest."

"Did your parents dying set you free?" I asked.

"I think them dying really helped," he replied. "It was like a major load came off my shoulders after that. It was like they no longer had much power over me and I could be free to be me. And even though I'd basically ended my relationship with them fifteen years before that, and pretty much thought I'd broken free from them, I didn't realize how much they still lived in my head and controlled my life. After they died I realized that just having known they were alive and out there in the world *had* affected me. I also realized that I'd still held on to a lot of guilt when they were alive—like I'd been letting them down. It really was a wake-up call for me to realize this, a shock—like, 'How in the world did I not figure this out when they were alive?' It was like I'd been blinded to some part of the reality. It really was mostly subconscious—and only popped into my consciousness when they were gone. And now I can say this with confidence: I really do feel fortunate that they died. To be honest, I didn't grieve them much at all. I'd done most of my grieving of them while they were still alive."

"Very interesting," I said.

"Yeah," he said. "So like I said, I really became more honest in my journaling after they died."

"Do you write a lot?" I asked.

"Yes and no," Terry replied. "I do write regularly, probably twice a week, but my journal entries are short and right to the point. I explore my feelings, their history, their context and their etiology. Basically, I write about my inner world as if I'm studying the behavior of a new sea anemone or jellyfish that's just been discovered by the scientific community. I write about everything I observe and I also try to make accurate sense of what all these phenomena mean. I've been doing this for years."

"So it sounds like you're writing a field guide about yourself."

"Exactly," he said, nodding, "except that I recognize that I, or at least what's going on in my head, is more complicated than any sea anemone and that what is 'me' is defined on multiple, subtle levels. I use my journal to tease out the motives and characteristics of the real *me* versus the wounded parts of my past, to separate the wheat from the chaff, as it were."

"How good are you at doing this?" I asked.

"Better than I used to be," he said. "Actually I think I'm pretty savvy at it now. I have some little bell inside me that rings true if I'm connecting with my authentic self. It's like I've gotten closer to having perfect pitch about who I am. And even now, when I don't have perfect pitch I can somehow feel that too. And journaling helps me sort it all out. I write out my whole process. And I've been doing it for years."

Chapter 12: Journaling, Part 2

Journals become powerful documents, not only for personal change but for larger change in the family system. In my journals I have written the most vulnerable and intimate things about myself and everyone and everything important in my life, past and present. My audience for my journals is me: my present and future self. Yet it is possible that our journals can also prove helpful to others.

Here I think of Erica, a thirty-year-old friend of mine who has a ten-year-old nephew named Joel. Joel is the son of Erica's older sister. Erica has a conflicted relationship with her sister and says she can only see her a few times a year, because she's so unpleasant toward her and critical of her for having broken away from their parents.

"The problem for me," said Erica, "is that I can't stand my sister but I love Joel. And it breaks my heart when I see how cruel she is toward him. She's got that kid wrapped so tight around her finger that he won't even eat an apple without asking her first. It really is a complete replication of her relationship with my mother—not that she sees it that way. But for me the real heartbreaker is how this is all affecting Joel. And I feel lousy that I can't spend more time with him."

"You can't just spend the day alone with Joel once in a while?" I asked.

"Are you kidding?" she replied with a smile. "My sister would never let me be alone with him! Part of her game is the notion that I'm not 'responsible enough.' It's really insane. I mean, I professionally lead children and teenagers on wilderness treks and have for the last eight years of my life. I'm state-licensed to do this, yet she says I'm not responsible enough to look after her child. She's destroying the kid's psyche but at the same time says I'm not responsible enough! She's already got him diagnosed with ADHD. It's sick and sad. And what makes it doubly sad for me is that Joel loves me to death. He'd kill to have a day alone with me. And deep down my sister knows that and that's why she keeps me away. She's jealous as all hell."

"And probably afraid," I added, "that you'll bond with him and sooner or later tell him what you think of her."

"Maybe," she said, "maybe true. And maybe she's right: I might say something honest to him about her. But before I did that I would have to be one hundred percent sure it was in Joel's best interest. If I wasn't thoroughly convinced it would help him I wouldn't say anything. But if it could help him, I'd say it."

"Yet it's really too much," I asked, "for you to spend more time with your sister and Joel together?"

"Yes," replied Erica. "It makes me feel ill to be around her and it really doesn't help Joel that much, because he and I can't have much honest exchange anyway, because she's always watching and intervening and 'putting limits' on everything. It doesn't change his basic situation at all. And then add to it that she inevitably makes comments about my relationship with our parents, and my 'hurtful attitude' toward them. It's really too much for me."

Erica then told me that she does, however, journal regularly and that through his journaling she realized a gift she *could* give Joel. In her journal she writes down every detail she sees, hears or remembers about Joel, especially about Joel's relationship with the key people in his life: Joel's parents. Erica writes down actual dialogue, she writes the ways in which her sister has manipulated Joel and she writes about Joel's father's passivity. Erica already sees how Joel has dissociated from many of his feelings, especially his anger, and Erica records that too.

"I'm saving this separate section of my journals for Joel, in case someday he wants to read it and learn about his history from my perspective. I've already got over eighty pages written about his life. Since he's already started blocking out what's happening to him I figure it might be really useful for him someday to know that someone out there was on his side and trying to keeping score about the truth of his childhood."

"Do you think he'll actually ever be up for reading it?" I asked.

"To be honest," Erica replied, "I don't know. My sister's really done a number on that kid's head. I mean, he's already on pills and everything for that fake diagnosis, but if he wants a roadmap out, I'm gonna help him find it. After all, I got away from my sick parents and I would have loved a document like this, even from someone who only saw me a few times a year. So you never know: maybe someday Joel will want it."

Interestingly, a few years ago I was going through a box of old family photographs and I found a snippet of words from my mother, written on a scrap of paper, that somehow ended up in there. They were dated from the summer of 1977, when I was five years old. In it she wrote, "Daniel was remarkably relaxed and happy. I didn't discipline him all day."

Although these lines might seem innocent enough, reading them had a big effect on me—because of their context. First, they reminded me of something I had forgotten: how my mother told me and everyone how anxious (that is, not "relaxed") of a child I often was. To her I was a socially problematic kid. I heard that refrain from her, in one form or other, throughout my whole childhood. She tried to compensate for it by telling me how "special" I was, but the negative stuff she labeled me with stuck in my head and hurt. Second, those written words reminded me that what she didn't tell anyone was what she couldn't admit: that some big part of my anxiety came directly from her. She induced it in me through her dishonesty, her obsessions, her perversity and her neglect of me. What sickened me in her journal entry was realizing that back when she had full power over me her way of dealing with my anxiety, the anxiety she caused, was to "discipline" me, that is, to punish me.

In reading that twelve-word journal entry of sorts I felt an overwhelming empathy for the little boy who was me and a cold repulsion for the person who had crushed me. I appreciated that entry: it was just another tiny, but at the same time large, confirmation for me what I had long since felt about her. I only wish I had had more of her writing to read. It would have helped me validate my feelings and my past even better. But alas, all I had was one snippet.

But what if reading more of her journal had overwhelmed me?

Sometimes parents' journals do overwhelm their adult child. John Prine documents this best in his presumably fictional song *Six O'Clock News*, in which a kid, Jimmy, surreptitiously reads his mother's diary, learns that he was the product of her one-night stand with a stranger and then kills himself.[13]

While I have no personal experiences of that degree of intensity, I do have one moderately intense story. Some years back I met a forty-year-old woman named Jessica who found me through my website. She had recently inherited an odd possession: twenty years of her father's journals, from the time before she was born right up until his death of a heart attack when she was twelve. She said she had not yet opened them and was frightened not only of what she might find inside but of how it might affect her. She asked my opinion.

---

[13] This was on John Prine's debut album (titled *John Prine*) from 1971. It's a great album.

I urged her to delve into them gently and slowly—when and if she felt ready. Although I didn't hide that if they had been from my father's pen they would have been like gold to me, I acknowledged that they could be emotionally risky for her, perhaps as gold was to King Midas.

Some weeks later Jessica emailed me back and told me that with both curiosity and trepidation she had taken the plunge and started perusing them. She stated that the entries had seemed pretty mundane—about her father's daily activities and work—until she found one that was all about his perspective on his relationship with her.

"It was cruel," she wrote. "And it made me nauseated. Although he was angry at me in the entry, it clearly went beyond momentary anger. I could just feel that he didn't care much about me. No one who cared about me would or could have written that way. It was like I was nothing to him— nothing of high value. I could only read a little bit more of it after that, and that was enough. It was then that I realized that I'm not a masochist. I don't need to take in any more of that crap. I'm going to have them all destroyed."

"Ah!" I wrote. "I mean, in one sense I hear you. You started out by reading some really intense stuff. It would totally stress me out if I read writing like that by my father, and I've been analyzing my relationship with him for years. But still, maybe it's worthwhile to hold on to them for a bit. They might become valuable to you someday. Or maybe you have a safe person in your life who could read parts of them for you—like a scout?"

"I don't think so," she replied. "But I appreciate what you say."

I next heard from Jessica a couple of years later.

"I just wanted to tell you," she wrote, "that I finally got rid of those journals—last week. I took them to a professional document shredder and I watched him feed them into the machine, one by one."

"All of them?" I asked in my reply email, trying to hide my feelings of disappointment.

"Yes, all of them," she replied. "I had stared at them in my closet for long enough—and finally made up my mind. I had no need for them anymore. They were bringing me down. Sometimes it's time to grow up and move on. I couldn't live with my father's burden hanging over me my whole life. I wanted a life of my own."

I didn't challenge Jessica on this, because I saw that she had taken an irreversible action. By destroying those journals she had destroyed a most valuable document. And although she spared herself the temporary pain, and probably, to be fair, a *very long-term* temporary pain, of having access into a polished window in her own history, in my opinion she also cut off a major avenue for breaking more deeply free from her parents. She felt she had moved on, but what I saw was that her actions had helped cement the foundation of her history into place—deep into her unconscious. It's like having a knotted hairball in your shower drain: if you don't pull it out it goes in deeper into the guts of the system and clogs everything worse. If you don't resolve your unconscious there is no way to move on.

I did, however, have one more question for Jessica.

"Do you yourself journal?" I asked her.

"Hell no!" she replied. "No way. I learned that lesson the hard way from my father. I write 'thank you' cards, Christmas cards, birthday cards, emails, an occasional Easter greeting and shopping notes. That's enough for me."

Chapter 13: Friendship

A friend is an ally, and we all need allies on this journey through life. Most of us grew up in childhoods that failed to provide us with deep allies. Our parents were not really on our side, not at the deepest levels and not for our sake first, and our childhood companions were often so ensnared in their own family dramas that they could only offer us limited support. We yearned for people to see us, believe in us and encourage us, but where were these people?

Before I found my first real friend, the only true relationship I had was my inner relationship with myself. When I was younger and that relationship was tenuous, I was so alone. This loneliness distorted my view of the world, leading me to the mistaken belief that no other person could ever deeply value me for me. As a child I developed a keen sense of radar to determine how much of my authenticity was safe to express at any given time. When I determined that people weren't totally safe I instead presented them with varying degrees of fake parts of myself—the parts that I had rehearsed and been rewarded for, or simply accepted for, in my family system. I could be witty, clever, mean, shallow, sarcastic, funny, super-empathic, silent, cynical or even at times bullying. These all garnered a better response from most people than being fully myself.

Yet my first deeply true friend, whom I met when I was 27, challenged these dynamics. His challenge, however, was not in any active sense of the word "challenge," rather, he just liked me when I was real. I could feel it. He mirrored to me, through no action other than being himself and respecting me, that the best of my internal relationship with myself could be transferred onto my external relationships with others. This was a revelation to me, because before I met him I hadn't known for sure if such a thing were possible. This not only comforted my heart but gave me hope for humanity. After all, if he could see me and like me for me, so too could others.

He, or I should say, my relationship with him, also challenged the negative things that my parents taught me about relationships. From my parents I learned that relationships, romantic or platonic, were inherently difficult and stressful and "all about compromise." I saw fighting, I saw emotional backstabbing, I saw gossip, I saw hurt feelings, I saw broken promises, I saw squelched feelings, I saw silence and I saw a lot of shutting down of hopes and dreams. And I also saw long periods of seeming normalcy, where all of this was hiding under the surface and I was lulled into believing all was okay. From my new friend I learned the opposite: that a relationship could be easy, devoid of deep stress, dynamic and growth-oriented and *not* related to compromising the things I valued most. In fact, our friendship worked in no small part *because* we both refused to compromise our values.

From my parents I learned that relationships got ugly if they became too intimate. They taught me, by example, that people were often dishonest, capricious and petty with themselves and others — and never admitted it. They taught me that people blamed you for their own flaws and could be cruel if you threatened their denial. From my new friendship I found another person who valued a true relationship with himself above everything—and self-reflected spontaneously, without any prompting from me. He admitted his flaws, amended his behavior and could talk about anything. Yet interestingly he had few flaws—because he had done a lot of inner work prior to meeting me. This was a major plus. He had good boundaries. He was largely aware of his unresolved childhood needs and didn't put them on me. He didn't expect me to take care of him in any way—because he was taking care of himself. In short, he was very open and honest, but without being needy. Suddenly I found a relationship that didn't leave me feeling frustrated, annoyed, violated, bored or hopeless. Here I had found someone whom I dared call an equal.

From my parents I learned that I was "grandiose" and "arrogant" if I admitted feelings that were too positive about myself. From my new friend I learned the opposite: that I was actually healthy to hold myself in positive, that is, realistic, regard. Self-love and self-respect were not threatening acts in our friendship. My parents were threatened by my true self. My friend liked me for me.

From my parents I learned that I was "judgmental" if I expressed my critical thinking too clearly or accurately—especially if it was about them or about people who were like them, that is, most people. They scorned and rejected me for my "judgmental nature." My new friend, however, confirmed the opposite: that I actually had very good judgment and that a human being I respected could actually like me more for expressing it openly. And I liked his good judgment too. I considered it one of his best qualities. It made for safe, deep conversation—not one laden with minefields and quicksand and pressure on me to try to read his mind before I spoke.

From my parents I learned that I was "selfish" and "intolerant" and "somehow defective" in relationships. From my new friend I learned that my authentic *self* was just fine, that I was perfectly healthy to be intolerant of people who rejected my authenticity and that what they labeled a defect was actually the positive mutation on which I had a chance to build an entirely new life. And what was amazing was that I trusted him. His integrity, his consistency and his insight earned that and continued to reinforce it at deeper levels.

From my parents I learned that I was somehow "deficient" and "abnormal" because I had never had "real" friends. They had drilled this into me so repeatedly that it became a painful subject in my life, in part because it had been true: I had always lacked for "real" friends. Yet I learned from the vantage point of my new friendship that no one in my family had *ever* had real friends either. I could now admit to myself that their so-called friendships—and most people's so-called friendships— were shallow and based largely on emotional lies. And I also learned that they had even lacked what I *had* always had, which was the precursor to true friendship: the root of an honest, self-reflective relationship with my inner self. I now realized better than ever why they pathologized me: my realness, and my struggle to keep my realness alive, terrified them, because it highlighted not just their limitations but also their denial of it. I had always been a threat to them and now that I had a real friend I became an even bigger threat.

And finally, from my parents, I learned that I was too "weird" and "strange" to ever be in a real romantic relationship. Something about me didn't match with the women I was attracted to, no matter how hard I tried. From my first friend I learned something new: that friendship was definitely the precursor to romance. And from this I realized that I had always been missing true friendship in my romantic relationships. And it wasn't for lack of trying: I simply had never found any girlfriend who had the qualities of a deep, appropriate friend for me. And I also grew to see —painfully—that I did not bring those qualities into my relationships with them. I instead had done the typical "male thing"—which I learned from both my parents, father *and* mother—of putting sexuality and emotional neediness first. Both, I came to realize, were a great mistake.

As the result of my friendship I became celibate. I now knew the minimum emotional qualities I needed in a romantic partner. And, to my surprise, this freed me up to seek women as real friends, which proved to be a boon in my life—not to mention practice for a solid part of what would someday be the most important part of any romantic relationship I might have.

Yet my new friendship wasn't all peaches and roses for me, because my new friend also saw how toxic I was in my relationship with my family.

He noticed how I engaged in unhealthy ways with them. And he didn't like it—because it impinged on our friendship. And he told me so, bluntly and directly—yet respectfully, with the good boundaries that his years of inner work had provided him. This came as a cup of cold water in my face: it woke up me. Through him I realized even more clearly how sadly sick they had made me and how sick I still remained. In spite of all the work I'd done up to that point I was still trying to win their love and I was doing it in ugly, self-disrespecting ways. And so I began a process of pulling back from them more than ever before. This was actually extremely painful for me, but it thrust my self-therapy process forward immeasurably.

Meanwhile, this all happened, or at least was well underway, more than ten years ago. These days my first friend and I are still the best of friends and in fact are even better friends now, because we have both grown both as individuals and allies. I grew out of many of my older and less healthy relationships in his company and he did the same. I changed my career and my life and so did he. And we both grew far more courageous and public in our lives. Our friendship gave each of us the confidence to share our lessons and insights at a broader level. We began to share the wealth —which has brought its own rewards. One for me is that I now have many other new friends in my life. And I love this.

Meanwhile, not infrequently people who are very lonely and isolated email me asking how they should go about finding or making friends. I wish I had an easy answer for every one of them, but my basic answer, perhaps not surprisingly, is this: become really good friends with yourself first. Try to develop the healthiest relationship with yourself that you can. Also, don't expect immediate perfection in your friendships. Maybe even having some good 'activity friends' could be a good start—people who share common interactive interests, like sports or movies or music or art or politics or books. Being good at interacting is a learnable skill, though for some people it takes a long time to develop.

The good news I have come to realize is that it is now easier than ever for people to find real friends in the world. I see the internet as a profound tool for connecting the rare breeds of true people with other true people. I was lucky to have met my friend at all, because we met in person in the late-1990s when the web was nothing resembling the phenomenon it is today. Yet we were more than just lucky, because we both lived in New York City, one of the biggest and most evolved, diverse and therapeutically-oriented cities in the world. Had I stayed in my little hometown in Upstate New York or even in my college city of Philadelphia the odds would have been stacked much more against me.

Nowadays people on the other side of the world can become deep and real and supportive friends through common interests, common websites and common philosophies with the help of Skype and other free social media applications. I myself have met many of my new friends—wonderful, real friends—through my website and my other social media channels. And people find me through all sorts of odd ways—even through keyword searches on search engines. I still find this amazing.

Presently I have my home base in New York City. Although I have a small number of real friends here my friendships are no longer bounded by the Hudson River and the East River and by the Bronx, Brooklyn, Queens and Staten Island. The world is now my friendship palette and I have people all over the world whom I love and who love me. I even have some friends with whom I communicate through Google Translate. Lack of a common language is no longer even such a limiting factor.

And I see this with others. Communities of like-minded and like-spirited people, people who are breaking with their families, are beginning to spring up around the world—real geographical communities and certainly very real internet communities. This is exciting, especially when I consider that these are the early days. Real people—people with that nexus of truth within their breast, that kernel of conscious connection with the truth of their spirit—are everywhere, and slowly they're having a chance to connect more easily than ever with others. I am hopeful that within a few years, and almost certainly within decades, these webs of connection will grow profoundly and allow everyone who has the hunger for growth to do so that much more easily.

And that's the key: it's easier to grow real in the company of others. We are a social species. We need others to see us. We get crushed in the crucibles of our sick families and until we break out and create a new social context we stay crushed. Yet if we break out of the parental orbit without having a new social network to hold us—and to hold our terror, pain, self-doubt and nervous hope—we find ourselves at major risk. We become the lone wolves who wander the frozen tundra without food or shelter or a protective circle. We risk emotional starvation and death. Going it alone for years really is too hard for many people, myself included. I made it to 27 on my own and it was so often a hellish journey. Girlfriends didn't help, old college friends didn't help, twelve-step programs didn't help, the mental health field didn't help and good work colleagues didn't help. I suffered in silence, because when I spoke no one really understood what I was talking about.

It is no surprise that many people who try to break from their families either run back to the family when the going gets rough (which I've done several times), replicate new family-like relationships based on sick, unconscious templates of childhood (which I've tried to do many times) or just commit suicide or live in the suicidal hopelessness of depression or addiction.

I am lucky that I did not kill myself. Although I never really considered suicide in any serious way, I did at some points have fleeting thoughts of ending my life. There were so many years where I found it terribly hard to hold on to hope—hope that someday I would be comfortable in my own real skin, hope that someday I would have companions with whom to share my journey and hope that someday I could have a real conversation with someone who would take my side and not revert to the default position of supporting the insanity of those who birthed and warped me.

So this brings me to my hope for the world: friendship and more friendship. Interlocking alliances of friendship groups. New cultures springing from conglomerations of friends. New societies based on truth, hope, honesty, boundaries, emotional depth, caring and growth. I see our world as existing at the very beginning of something new. Ten years ago I did not see it. Now I see it because I live it—in little pieces, in little pockets, bit by bit. Every day I see an increasing number of people who want to break from their families and try something new—not always with a full commitment, but often with a spark of a feeling, with an idea, with a hope of something better. I see people with something to offer others and a willingness to receive from others. Sometimes this willingness expresses itself clumsily and sometimes the friendships that spring from it are rocky, but these the early days. I see us, in a sense, as mutants: new people trying new things, exploring new ways of being, making occasional mistakes in replicating unhealthy family dynamics, but striving for newness nonetheless—and learning all the while.

I see more and more people coming to grips with reality, and that excites me. These people call me. They email me. They post comments on my internet videos. They write words of thanks and encouragement on my website. They invite me into their homes when I travel. And sometimes they're randomly sitting next to me on an airplane or bus or subway. We talk—and I realize that the pulse of the world is changing.

Ten years ago I wouldn't have considered writing this book, because I wouldn't have thought there was an audience for it.

Now I know there is one. It may not be a united community yet, but it's there. And it's growing.

Chapter 14: Therapy

Therapy can be very helpful and also very hurtful. In the best situation, you find a psychotherapist who has already broken from the sick sides of his parents and intuitively sides with your inner child. He can look under the surface of the adult self you present and see the remnants of your unloved, untended, unhealed and needy child. In the worst situation, which, from what I have observed, is common, you find a therapist who hasn't broken all that deeply from his parents, unconsciously sides with them, by extension sides with yours and largely pathologizes you for wanting to break away. This is devastating, because it essentially reduces your supposedly therapeutic relationship to a dynamic in which you pay a parental surrogate to drill into you the same messages that damaged you as a child and sent you into therapy in the first place.

It doesn't help that the psychotherapy field in general has backward goals. The field largely tends to focus its energy and its mission not on guiding people closer to their authentic selves but on bringing happiness, that is, dissociative comfort, at all costs. The field focuses not on deep healing but on the reduction of such so-called "symptoms" as depression, anxiety, panic, grief, insecurity and anger. The problem here is that these symptoms, as painful as they may be, are our friends: they are our psyche's way of telling us that something is wrong and that we have a desperate desire to heal. Reducing symptoms without solving the underlying problem is contrary to healing. In practical terms this translates into pressuring people to make peace with their abusive parents, to bury the feelings their parents induced in them and, in so doing, to become abusers themselves. The field fails to see that depression, however dysfunctional it renders the people experiencing it, is actually a healthier psychological stage than dissociative comfort, that the pain and misery associated with grieving is the only doorway into real emotional health and that anxiety, insecurity and anger are normal byproducts of resolving trauma and growing.

Great therapists understand the value in grieving, because they have personal experience being there and coming out the other side. They know how terribly we all wanted and deserved perfect parents as children and they know how devastating it is to let go of this desire and accept adult responsibility for ourselves. They have suffered through the pain of their loneliness, worked through their history of abandonment, acknowledged their losses and ultimately found themselves. They have done their own inner homework and in so doing have solidified a strong, clear, mature, independent identity. They may not have done this perfectly, in every ounce of their being—in fact, no one I know has done this perfectly—but they have done a lot. This makes them strong, real and clear-seeing. This not only allows them to differentiate your core of inner truth from the voices implanted in you by your family, but puts them squarely on the side of your inner child.

A great therapist actually loves your little inner child and is willing to fight like hell for him or her. If he doesn't then he's a quack and should give you your money back.[14] In this vein, all three of the therapists I saw were quacks. I will share about the first two now, then the third afterward. The first two both behaved with seeming neutrality toward me. No matter what I shared, they just sat there and stared at me, occasionally asking more questions, getting me to reveal my most painful vulnerabilities and never taking sides. At first I thought they were neutral; now I realize they were neutered—and profoundly on the side of my parents. Regardless of my level of understanding at the time, their behavior tortured me, because unconsciously I realized—and vividly I felt—that they certainly weren't on the side of my wounded child. And later, when I realized this consciously, I became furious because I knew I had been cheated.

Unlike my first two therapists, great therapists open their hearts to you and give you the best of their minds, their personalities, their experience, their patience, their self-reflections, their point of view and their emotions. I know a few special therapists out there. I see how far they go to fight for the child within their client. Their work for them is more than a job: it is a calling, and an exhausting one. It is no job to leave at work at the end of the day. Many people naïvely think that therapists shouldn't get too personally involved with their clients. This is rubbish. Good therapists get in there and get their hands dirty. They let you into their lives. The way they let you in is by forming a real, flesh-and-blood, emotional

---

[14] The reality that I've observed, however, is that getting one's money back from a therapist because he or she was psychologically blind is probably not realistic. I've actually never seen it happen. I've heard of people confronting therapists about this, though, and even demanding money back, but I've never heard of it working. Instead my observation is that the act of trying to win money back from a bad therapist is more often that not triggering and potentially retraumatizing.

relationship with you. This relationship harbors an exchange of feelings, vulnerabilities and humanity. When you pay them money, you pay not just for their advocacy but for their camaraderie and their insight and their caring on your journey through life. They will get to know you, and you will get to know them as well.

A real therapist values your questions, your anger, your sorrow, your traumas, your grief, your wounded sides, your beauty, your strength, your weaknesses and most especially your wounded little child. Your therapist values these things in you because he values these same things in himself. He has walked the walk, he continues to walk the walk and now he is willing to be patient as you walk it too. But that does not mean that he will accept anything. This relationship, after all, is not a fake relationship; he too has his limits. He wants you to grow more than anything and if he sees that you are not fighting properly for yourself this will trouble him. He will let you know and you will feel it. How he expresses this, however, relates to the question of both his gentleness and his sense of timing. Like a good musician, he knows when to play his instrument and when to rest silently.

But how do you assess a therapist's quality? How do you know if a therapist is good or not? I get emailed these questions all the time, sometimes several times a week. People read my website and watch my internet videos and want me to assess their therapist for them. Although I can often surmise certain things about a therapist from the details that people email me, usually the sole fact that they are reaching out to me on the subject signifies that there is something wrong, and usually quite wrong, with their therapist. After all, good therapists earn their clients' trust and help them not just to present their questions in session but to resolve them there as well. Also, from what I have observed, by the time most people reach out to me with their questions they have given up hope for the therapy and want an outsider with some seeming objectivity to validate it.

And I understand this sentiment well. When I was last in therapy I probably would have emailed someone like myself had I found a website like mine. My third and final therapist was awful. I ended up feeling trapped in a twice-weekly therapy relationship with her, desperately hoping she would see me, doing everything I could to reveal my authentic self so she would take my side, deluding myself at times into believing that she did see me yet repeatedly finding my hopes dashed when I awoke to reality. I so wanted her to love me, that is, to love my wounded little child. That was the glue that kept me in therapy and it was the exact same glue that had kept me tied to my parents as a child and as an adult. I just transferred the glue from them to her.

Interestingly, this is exactly what I was supposed to be doing in therapy, except that I was doing it with the wrong therapist. She was inappropriate because she lacked an ability to help me sort out my dynamics, because she didn't understand them. She hadn't sorted out this level of emotional material in her own life and her own history. So instead she encouraged these dynamics in me. For instance, although at first I found her to be an excellent listener, in time I realized that she also used her skill as a silent listener to hide her opinion, which I came to consider an incorrect opinion, of me. This precisely replicated my relationship with my mother, because, like my mother, she wouldn't acknowledge what she was doing or thinking. My therapist kept silent—and her therapeutic training told her this was not just acceptable but appropriate. Yet how was I supposed to heal from my relationship with my mother in a relationship with a person who behaved in almost the exact same way?

What tortured me about this, though, was that: (1) my therapist said, at least early on in our relationship when she talked more freely, that I *could* heal from my relationship with my mother through my "analytic" relationship with her, and (2) she said, later in the relationship, when she talked much less, that the resistance to this healing *was mine*.

This put the power of knowledge, correctness, maturity and insight entirely on her side of the relationship and the vulnerability, the unsureness, the confusion and the immaturity entirely on my side. According to her, *she knew the right way and I didn't,* and if I wanted to grow I had to trust her, even though she hadn't earned my trust and had in fact earned my distrust. This again replicated my relationship with my mother, a relationship in which I had to sell myself out in order to get loved.

This therapy trapped me—emotionally—for eighteen months. I felt desperate to confirm my suspicion that she was not on my side, because somehow, deep down in my authentic self, I knew exactly where she stood. And I have since learned this in life: our authentic self knows everything and so can we *if* we listen to it. The problem for me back then was that I wasn't so clear on the difference between my authentic self and the sick, implanted voices of my parents that bounced around in my head. I see this as very common with many people who are in the midst of breaking up with their parents. It can be very hard to know who exactly we really are—and what exactly is our core of truth—especially when we are under a lot of pressure. In my case, I couldn't reliably trust my own instincts because my parents' voices constantly shouted them down. That actually is why I was in therapy in the first place. The problem is, my therapist's instincts were even more muddled than mine.

Thankfully I figured this out on my own, primarily through journaling and bouncing ideas off a few trusted friends and secondarily through assiduously grilling her to figure out her point of view. I was a very assertive therapy client and this saved my life. Psychologically I analyzed everything she said (or dared to say) in order to figure out her logical inconsistencies. For months at a time she retreated into almost complete silence as a result and I analyzed that too. And through all of this, in spite of her and her sickness and her denial, my analysis bore fruit and I became stronger and more trusting of my authentic self. For me it was a time of psychological isometric exercise. I pushed and pushed and pushed, she didn't budge an inch and all the while I grew stronger anyway.

And once I did figure out her point of view and become strong enough to admit to myself that she wasn't able to care about the deepest part of me and likely never would—and therefore really had little to offer me—I managed to extricate myself from the relationship. But the process leading up to this was hellish and quite parallel to breaking from my parents. She gave me no support and instead actively pathologized me for leaving, saying that I was quitting early, that I was afraid to face my feelings, that my lack of commitment to therapy signified my lack of commitment to myself and to my growth process and that I was taking the easy way out. The implication in all this was that she was healthy and that I was not. And during the final months of therapy this was hard for me to sort out, because in part she was right: *I wasn't entirely healthy.* I *was* projecting some of my unresolved childhood material onto her and I had grown attached to her, or at least to the fantasy that she could somehow love me and help me and guide me. And how could I have avoided it? The whole way she set up our therapy relationship, with her as the silent, knowing, money-receiving guru and me as the revealing, unknowing, paying patient, encouraged projection and did nothing to resolve it.

In hindsight, though, I realize she was probably projecting as much onto me as I was onto her, if not more—and also more intractably so because she lacked an ability to study it. I saw no evidence that she was engaged in an honest, internal dialogue with herself of the variety that I had and was improving upon daily. I suspect that to her my quitting therapy represented, on an unconscious level, both her parents' abandonment of her and her desperation to break away from them. Both of these things terrified her and in order to keep her terror under wraps, the wraps that kept her life in the stable order of normalcy, she did all within her power to keep me hooked in the relationship. That was why she fought me so hard and with such absolutely passive resistance. We were locked in a death grip with each other: I trying desperately to wake up and wake her up so she could help me, and she trying desperately to numb me out so I would stop threatening her slumber. I'm sure this was hell on her, yet that was not my problem. The hell she was going through in relation to me was hers to worry about. And when I had therapy relationships with clients that were in some ways emotionally hellish on me I was very clear both to myself and with them that *this was not their problem*. This was my problem. After all, they weren't paying me to take care of me and my feelings!

Meanwhile, looking back with the hindsight of more than a decade, I realize now that I probably would have been a much better therapist *for* my therapist than she was for me. Had the roles been reversed I think I could have empathized with her and nurtured her growth process—and her breakup process with the sick sides of her parents, both her actual parents and the parents embedded in her head—far better than she nurtured mine. Of course, I would have behaved totally differently toward her had our 45-minute sessions been on her dime instead of mine. I would have been gentle, patient and caring toward her—which I wasn't as her client, because I knew it was not in my best interest to do so; it was my job to grow at all costs. That is the job of a therapy client. However, I find it interesting at times to speculate on these hypothetical role reversals. Of course, at the time I was in therapy with her I wasn't wasting my energy on these thoughts. I was fighting for my growth—for my emotional survival.

Yet, strangely, for all I say about the negatives of that therapy, it did provide me some valuable gifts. For starters, I learned a lot about my right to be angry at people who took on a role of great responsibility in my life yet were defrauding me. I also learned a lot about sticking up for myself —and being bluntly honest—in the face of stonewalling denial. I didn't realize this until years later, but in a strange way, in spite of all my therapist's uselessness, my relationship with her gave me a good template for breaking away from the people who once had been a lot more important to me than she herself could ever have been.

I also learned a lot from my relationship with her, in a very intimate way, about bad therapy. This provided me some invaluable lessons about what *not* to do as a therapist with my own clients. It also provided me a strong vaccination against returning to bad therapy. It also helped me gain an extra dose of empathy for my future clients, which I put to good use when they told me stories about the atrociousness and hypocrisy of their past therapists. I heard these stories all the time; for every one story I heard about a great past therapist I probably heard a hundred about a charlatan. My therapist, after all, was not that unusual as far as therapists go. She behaved how anyone would behave if they'd never broken deeply from their parents and held the power position in the relationship with a person who was going through the parental breakup process.

I also learned a lot, during my time with her, about what genuine therapy was, because I was actually doing it: on my own. *I had to do it* to prevent her from driving me crazy. All that journaling I did was genuine therapy. All the self-reflecting I did in the company of my new friends was also therapy. All the dream analysis I did was genuine. And therein my growth happened. And ultimately this taught me a lesson, which I shared repeatedly with my own future therapy clients: the real way to be in therapy is to do self-therapy. Formal therapy with a formal therapist, be he me or anyone, is at best an adjunct to the more important inner work that you do with yourself, by yourself. The real growth happens inside of you, with your authentic self at the helm. You guide it and your motivation propels it forward. An external therapist, at best, comes along for the journey as a consultant and helps smooth the path and perhaps lighten your load a bit. And when you get strong enough to do for yourself what the therapist previously did for you, you move along on your own. It really is parallel to growing up and leaving home.

All this said, I rarely recommend that people go to a therapist, in large part because I know so few excellent therapists for referral. If I do not know of an excellent therapist I do not recommend therapy. The reason for this is that my experience has taught me that when it comes to the deep issues of breaking from parents and from the family system, therapists who are not excellent, that is, therapists who do not have a firm grasp of these dynamics intellectually and who do not deeply embody them in their actual emotional lives, are simply not competent. And this makes them dangerous. They really can hurt people. I feel lucky I escaped that last therapist's clutches. Heaven forbid I had been less strong and gotten stuck. It happens all the time.

But what about other forms of therapy, like family therapy and group therapy? To reply bluntly, I am wary of them. My wariness with family therapy comes because too often it strays into treating the whole family as the client. This risks minimizing your inner child's truth in order to accommodate your parents' feelings, and all the more so to the degree that the family therapist unconsciously sides with your parents' denial, which seems par for the course with most family therapists. And although I have heard of some people who have used therapists as referees for directly confronting their parents, which can potentially be useful if the therapist has clearly defined himself as being on your side and not theirs, all too often family therapy sends you a much more conventional message of compromise, acceptance and forgiveness.

My wariness of group therapy comes because I've never seen it be useful it helping people break from their parents in a healthy way. And I've seen a lot of the opposite. Too many group therapists I know and have heard about love playing the guru role, the parental-like leader of the flock. Some group therapists I've heard of are comfortable helping a client break from his parents without breaking from the parents embedded in his psyche. They assist him in replacing his family of origin with the therapy group, with themselves at the head. These groups are cults; they replace the cult of the family of origin with new people. These are of course to be avoided, though many people in their desperation for community and mirroring fail to spot them. But more often than not group therapy is mundane in its goals: it reinforces, in a peer-pressuring environment, the same old messages of the value of the family of origin and does not foster any great degree of emotional exploration or separation from parents.

So if it sounds like I'm fairly skeptical of therapy in general, it's true: I am. For years I have told people, especially those with what would conventionally be defined as an "extreme goal" of wanting to break away not just from their parents but from the parents in their psyches, that if they cannot locate an excellent therapist they're probably better off saving their money and doing self-therapy instead, especially if they have the motivation. On the other hand, if they are in therapy already, or want to try therapy anyway, I often recommend the following:

1) Ask your therapist a lot of questions. Bring in any important questions you have and ask them. Don't wait. And if your therapist doesn't like your questions or criticizes you for asking too much then you may have saved yourself a lot of future time and money, because you have found out that he or she is not good enough.

2) Do your own self-therapy concurrently. Journal. Analyze your dreams. Self-reflect as much as you can. Surround yourself with the most healing, growing, maturing people you can find and engage with them to the best of your ability. Grow as much as you can on your own and with unpaid others, so that you don't end up falling into a trap of becoming

overly emotionally dependent on your therapist. Thus, if he or she does not prove to be helpful this makes it easier for you to leave.

3) Be assertive in therapy. Challenge your therapist anytime you feel like it. This is okay. Be wary of lying down on the couch and staring up at the ceiling. (I did a lot of this; it's probably rarely a good idea. By design it encourages projection. It's like talking on the phone or emailing with someone versus meeting with them in person. Face-to-face interaction grounds the interaction in much more reality.) Look your therapist in the eye. Study his or her reactions. Comment on those reactions. Share your own reactions. Have a human relationship with your therapist. And if your therapist can't handle this or doesn't see this as a valuable thing to work toward then you will have hopefully learned a valuable lesson: time to leave.

4) Get outside opinions from others about your therapy. Ask your most trusted and mature friends and allies what they think of your therapy. And bring their opinions into therapy. My therapist did not like it that I spoke with others about what happened in our private therapy sessions. She felt I was "leaking the therapy," the implication being that I was betraying her. The thing is, I *was* betraying her in a sense: I was betraying her betrayal of me! As such, I consider therapists who demand privacy to be sick because they are replicating the major family taboo of "don't break family secrets." The reality is this: clients can and often are wise to share whatever they want from the therapy office with whomever they choose,

as publicly as they wish. Only the therapist is incumbent to maintain confidentiality.

5) Solicit the therapist's opinion. Find out what the therapist is thinking. Request transparency. Put them on the spot. That's what you're paying them for! If you feel uncomfortable then speak about it. Open up. Be communicative. That is one of the wonderful things about good therapy: it's a place that is safe for you to communicate exactly who you are, what you are feeling and what is troubling you. Thus, if your therapist does not support your desire to communicate freely in session then your therapist is not wonderful and will probably not help you much. Your therapist, after all, should be an expert (or at least pretty damn good!) at healthy, open communication. That's what a real therapist is.

6) Take your therapy seriously. Show up on time. Make sure you get your full session. Get a good night of sleep before your session. Prepare for your session beforehand however you see fit. Do whatever it takes to make your therapy a high priority in your life, because it *is* a high priority. And demand a therapist who shares this attitude. You deserve a therapist who takes your healing as seriously as you do. You're not paying them to be a passive observer of your life. You deserve a real professional in your corner, someone who can best help catalyze your growth process.

Chapter 15: Confronting Parents, Part 1

Confronting parents is a complicated business. While breaking from your parents inherently entails taking distance from them, confronting them calls for doing the opposite: going toward them, and in some ways coming very close to them. For many people their moments of confrontation with their parents are the times in their lives, at least in their adults lives, where they step *the closest* to their parents. So in a way it might seem a bit contradictory to write about confronting parents in a book about breaking away from them. Yet I don't see it that way. So often confronting them, even if only mildly, can be a vital part, or even a stage, in the breaking away process.

In some ways the confrontation of parents by children reminds me of some aspects of couple's therapy. As a therapist who worked with a fair number of couples, I have learned that there are two basic outcomes of this therapy: (1) more closeness for the couple or (2) more separation, which often translates to splitting up, or, in the case of marriage, divorce. The couple's therapy tends to bring to the surface the primary issues of the relationship and give both members of the couple a chance to see what's going on both in their own and their partner's life, and of course in the relationship. And with that knowledge on the surface, witnessed publicly by all in the room, it's hard to sweep it under the carpet. In that way couple's therapy tends to be a confrontation of sorts: a confrontation of denial, a confrontation of hidden patterns, a confrontation of the meaning of silent messages and a confrontation of people's histories and real feelings. That closeness brings about changes, and often quite quickly.

Confronting parents is similar in that the result of the intense closeness is change, be it more closeness or more distance. In the context of this book, not surprisingly, the result is often more distance, though in the forthcoming chapters I do share some case examples where this is not the case. But the purpose of confrontation is not about closeness or distance, but discovery: discovery of who you are, how you feel around your parent or parents in this new context and what comes up within you and them. It is a chance to study your reactions, their faces, your memories, their defenses, your feelings afterwards, their tone of voice and of course your changing relationship with them and theirs with you. A confrontation, though inherently risky (as I shall explore through case examples), is a mine for treasure. The question in my mind is what kind of treasure you're seeking and how good of a miner you are.

If you choose to confront your parents, I believe that the wisest goal to aim for is your own personal growth. The way to do this is to confront them, your mother and father or either separately, from the perspective of an adult. Many people to one degree or another confront their parents from the perspective of a wounded child. What I mean by this is that they hold the secret childlike goals of (1) changing their parents, (2) rebuilding the parental bond and (3) making their parents love them more. This type of confrontation has some pretty high risks, first because it's a setup for failure. Unless your parents are absolutely rare individuals, the likes of which I have not seen, they are far too wounded and unconscious to be able to side with your inner child to any significant degree when the façade gets stripped away. And confrontations often are pretty good at façade-stripping.

From what I have observed, most parents have little capacity to side with your inner child. Also, if they were healthy enough to change so easily they would have already started a self-therapy process of their own, motivated entirely from within, which included confronting their own actual parents and internalized parents. Some parents have done this, and it speaks to their maturity, though sadly the degree of which most parents have done this tends to remain limited. But if they haven't done these things, which most haven't, it's unlikely they'll change in a positive way as the result of any confrontation. Also, few people, even fairly healthy people, grow much when they are under attack. Instead they hunker down, attack back and become more rigid and angry. In short, they'll feel like victims and blame you.

Yet ironically, even if they did grow it probably wouldn't help you much, because as an adult you have to take responsibility for yourself. For that reason, if you do have some hope of changing them and you can admit it to yourself it may prove wiser to hold off on confronting them and instead focus on your own self-therapy. But I want to make clear that even though it may be unwise to confront them if you are unconsciously doing so from the perspective of the child's needs, *you certainly have a right to confront them*. After all, you never asked to be abused, much less abused by the people who created your existence. So in terms of your rights I fully support you, but more so, *life* fully supports you. But in practical reality I hope you confront as wisely as possible. After all, the goal is to grow, not get burned. But ironically, even getting burned can provoke growth. Here I think of an old-growth redwood forest: sometimes only a high-heat forest fire will trigger seedlings to sprout.

I now wish to share the story of a friend of mine named Pete, age 39, a teacher who shared with me the story of his confrontation of his mother. I will devote the rest of the chapter to it, because it is profound.

"I've done some of my most serious emotional growth in a direction away from my parents," said Pete, "as the result of getting severely emotionally betrayed from having confronted them. This mainly happened when I was 33 and confronted my mother for, among other things, having repeatedly violated my sexual boundaries in my childhood. My inner work of many years prepared me, or at least I thought it prepared me, for this confrontation. I'd done so many hours of emotional processing around it, including dredging up disturbing memories, journaling, being in lots of therapy, grieving, sharing my history with friends, meditating—and doing a lot of confronting of my inner demons, many of which I realized were her voices that I'd swallowed up inside me. As the result of all this I felt strong enough to tell her exactly what she did to me and to let her know how much her sickness affected me. It was bursting out of me and I wanted her to know, in person, what I'd discovered about the reality of what she did to me and how it affected me."

"And she agreed to do it?" I asked.

"Yes," he replied. "She did. But let me backtrack a little. So, at first I called her up and confronted her on the phone. I told her I wanted to do it and she was okay with it. For a while she heard my confrontation, and cried a lot during it, but then she refused to talk with me more on the phone, saying she preferred to meet with me in person. I think it was just a ploy to get me to back out, because it was so emotionally intense for her. But somehow I couldn't back out. Although I felt nervous, as I hadn't seen her in like five years and didn't feel quite safe around her, I agreed and I drove over to her house in a suburb of Los Angeles and I confronted her in private, over a period of several hours. I had mentally prepared a list of about a hundred ways she had been sexually perverse with me and I slowly went down the list, almost as if I had her on trial."

"Damn," I said. "Intense."

"Yeah," he affirmed. "It was. So anyway, she came prepared: no crying, very defensive, very closed up. Very different from how she'd been on the phone. Instead she was more of her regular self: she admitted nothing and denied everything. She ducked my questions, she played word games with her answers, she showed no emotion whatsoever and, when she thought she could get away with it, she went on the attack and tried shifting the blame onto me—which was the regular pattern in my family. And it used to work pretty well back then in terms of getting me to shut up. But not this time. I really was a different person. Instead I ground away at her, trying to get her to remember, to acknowledge and to admit the truth—and to empathize with me. It was like we were in a game of chess, locked into it. And she was one heck of a player. She was formidable. In a sense she impressed me—with how tough and closed and dishonest she was."

"I can picture it in my mind."

"Yes," Pete said. "Yes! It's six years later and it's still burned into my head. So anyway, suddenly, after about an hour-and-a-half of her total denial of everything I was saying, a chink appeared in her armor. Up to that point I'd confronted her about parading around naked in front of me when my dad was off at work, of her telling me about intimate details of her sex life with my dad, about telling me detailed, private information about both of my younger sisters' puberty development, of her sleeping in the same bed with me when I was way too old for it and snuggling up to me, of her smoking marijuana and then telling me sexual stories from her teen years—all this crap that she shouldn't have been doing. But she denied it all, like it never existed. But then, in this one weird moment, when I was confronting her about her prying into my life when I was thirteen and trying to figure out if I masturbated—and even encouraging me to masturbate, and telling me how to do it—she suddenly and totally unexpectedly relented. She remembered. And she didn't deny it. She remembered—and admitted it. Not with words, but with a look. She nodded and admitted it."

"What happened next?" I asked.

"Well," he replied, "her face changed. Very obviously. She got this weird look on her face, this strange, strange look of truth—this look of being totally busted or caught or exposed. And she looked almost in shock. And horrified. And embarrassed. Yet *real* at the same time. This was the weirdest part for me. She looked—I hate to say this, but it was true—even beautiful. Like a lost and wounded little girl who was suddenly empathic to my point of view. It was the weirdest thing, that look—and what I can say now, but couldn't then, at that moment, was that that look of hers, that sad and strange and honest look, that was a look, an acknowledgment, that I *craved* from her. I craved her honesty. Her admission. Her truth. Her love. Her bowing down to reality. In that moment I had a mother who was on my side. I think I was just desperate for that look—and I hadn't admitted that to myself before I confronted her, because I hadn't known it. All my inner healing I'd done hadn't brought me to that realization of how much I still wanted her as a mother."

"I relate," I said. "I've been there, and in some ways, in some unhealed parts of me, I think I still am."

"Yes," he said. "I hear you. So anyway, when she had that look on her face, I lost it: I started to cry. My throat was tight and then my tears pouring out of me. And suddenly she got cold. It was like her spirit died. Her face lost its softness and I saw her taking everything back. And then she spoke. She said she thought that I remembered it wrong—and that it was actually me who brought up masturbation with her, that I had come to *her* for advice."

"Oh?" I asked.

"She was lying!" he replied. "That never happened. It was a total lie. She was lying to cover her memory, and she knew it. And I freaked out inside. It was then that I really lost it."

"What did you do?" I asked.

"Well," replied Pete, "I'm not proud to say it, but I slapped her. I stood up, I walked by her and I slapped her shoulder as I passed—not very hard, but hard enough to let her know how furious I was, and to let her know what a liar she was. I had never done anything like that to her in my life. I think I cursed at her too, called her a 'lying bitch' or something like that. I think I was in shock, or at least some sort of altered state. I then went to the bathroom, washed my face and came back out and joined her. I felt more normal then. Ninety percent calmer. I sat back down and continued crying, but quieter now. I offered to leave as the result of slapping her, but she told me she wanted me to stay. And then suddenly she started crying. Her tone went soft again. I guess something had shifted in her when I was in the bathroom. Her eyes went back to admitting the truth. So I stayed. And we talked for another two hours. And now her guard was dropped, and it stayed down. I didn't have to force anything. It actually was no longer like a confrontation. Now the conversation felt mutual, like some large piece of truth had bubbled up from within her, just like the truth was bubbling up from within me. We both cried then—really cried. We were actually sobbing. It was totally unexpected and unusual."

"Damn," I said. "This is so intense."

"Yeah," he said. "It was. We both sobbed like mad and in those two hours she admitted more to me about her past crimes against me than she had in my entire previous life. She acknowledged having behaved incestuously toward me and through all her tears she admitted that she'd had no business becoming a parent, that she had behaved inappropriately toward me and toward my sisters throughout my childhood, that she had been a rotten wife to my equally rotten father—whom she later divorced—that she had poisoned my relationship with my sisters and that she was deeply, deeply sorry. I mean, she was really sobbing. I'd never seen anything like it."

"Wow," I said. "Wow."

"Yeah," he said. "And what she ended with was this: 'I pray,' she said, still crying, her face all full of tears, 'that someday, Peter, someday you can find it in yourself to love me again. I don't expect it, but I hope you can. I am so sorry for what I did to you.'"

"How was it for you to hear that?"

"Well," he replied, "in a strange way it caused me to feel relief. I felt the confrontation had been so worth it. I also felt that with her newly expressed honesty we had found the potential to begin a new relationship, because now she was starting on a deep path toward growth. I felt like I had a mother again. And I told her this and she agreed. And as I got up to leave—nearly four hours after having arrived—we hugged deeply and I found the feeling to be oddly blissful. And not dissociated. And I remember asking myself after I hugged her and I walked back to my car, 'Do I really finally have a mother on my side? Have all my fantasies come true?' And I hadn't even known, really, that those were fantasies of mine. Talk about eye-opening."

"Yes. And intense."

"Yes. But anyway, let's put it this way: my bliss was short-lived. The next day, when she was back in the regular tracks of her regular life, back with her three cats and her dog and back with me out of the picture, she reverted to her old self and she blamed me. Full-on. She focused the blame on my slapping her, which she called 'a criminal assault,' and one of her friends emailed everyone in my close family, including my dad, who hated my mom, about what I'd done. And her friend threatened that my mother could have me arrested for what I'd done."

"Jesus," I commented.

"Yep," said Pete. "Yep. And to make matters worse, over time my mother changed the story into one where I'd punched her for no reason whatsoever—though I didn't find this out till later. She swapped it around so that she became the totally innocent female victim and I became the harmful male abuser. She labeled me a person with bizarre, inexplicable behavior, which was reminiscent of the tale she'd told about me my whole life. And, at least at first, everyone in my extended family sided with her. No one even asked me what had happened. They just believed her."

"Damn."

"Yep. But to be fair, despite her historical abuses of me, I *had* behaved like a child by slapping her. A very immature and wounded side of me had come out and I wasn't proud of it. This gross error—coming from my unresolved shit—had allowed her to turn the tables on the confrontation. So to make a long story short, I lived with the fear of being arrested for three years until the statute of limitations on felonious assault ran out. During that three-year period, though, in which I worked full-time at my school, I did a lot of soul-searching and came to some realizations. These realizations have been the gifts of my confrontation, because I have built a stronger, wiser self on them. I actually wrote them out, and I can read them to you if you wish."

"Sure," I replied. "I'm totally curious to hear them—if you're okay with it."

"I am," said Pete. "Yes. I feel this is important—and I feel glad to be able to share this. So, here it is:

'My first realization was that deep down, underneath all her surface protestations of love, and there were a lot of them, my mother did not have it within her to care about me, not in any deep, sustained way. Perhaps she loved me deep in her core somewhere, but the life she lived and the life she had long chosen gave her no access to her core. When she hinted at having me arrested to protect her denial, I saw in no uncertain terms the character of the person who created me and controlled my existence for my earliest, most powerless, more formative years. I finally was able to accept that she valued her dishonest relationship with herself more than she valued her honest relationship with me. This was a revelation to me. As unpleasant as this truth was, I found my acknowledgment and acceptance of it incredibly helpful and refreshing, because it confirmed some basic kernel of what my early childhood memories told me about her and my relationship with her.

'My second realization was that I no longer saw any point in confronting her again, because I had gotten my answer loud and clear: (a) that some powerful part of her is broken, (b) that she will likely always harm me deeply if she feels threatened and has access to me, and (c) that in all likelihood, no matter what I do or don't do, she will never change. I also realized that I would be delusional to want to continue my relationship with her. I also realized how delusional I had been my whole life for wanting a relationship with her. As a child, though, my delusions were

age-appropriate and to my benefit: had I had no delusional hope for her as a parent then I would not have gotten any love from her and without that love I would have shriveled and died like an abandoned infant.[15] So my insanity protected me then, because it insured the maintenance of whatever scraps of love she could and did offer me. But when I grew up those little scraps of love became an outdated limb: I didn't need them anymore. It just took me a while to figure it out.

'My third realization was that had I done some more dedicated inner work or inner healing before *confronting her I could have probably come to these same realizations without having put myself at risk of arrest. Arrest, jail, maybe even a trial would have been a horror for me, because she could have said anything to the police, and knowing her she probably would have. I could have lost my teaching license, because I was supposedly quite 'mentally imbalanced' and thus, according to some members of my family, professionally dangerous. My mother could have told the police the lie she told my family—that I'd physically wounded her —and my life could have changed in an instant.'"*

"So do you think," I asked, "you could have figured all this out without confronting her?"

---

[15] This reminded me of Rene Spitz's famous neglected Romanian orphans who were never touched or loved in their infancy, only fed and sterilely cleaned. For more about Spitz's work, and also Harry Harlow's isolation and separation experiments with baby monkeys, see Deborah Blum's 2002 book *Love at Goon Park: Harry Harlow and the Science of Affection* (Perseus Publishing).

"I think so," he replied. "I *do* think so. I'm not sure, but I think so. But what I know is that that knowledge—that knowledge that I am an adult who can really take care of myself and that I don't need a mommy anymore—that was always within me. Somehow I've always known it. I just didn't want to face it. I still wanted to run back to her. And that was part of my motive in confronting her, I think. Ugh—it sounds horrible to admit, but I think in some ways by confronting her I was begging her to love me again. And I was already well into my thirties by then. Begging her to make up for what she did to me and how she'd hurt me. And frankly that could never happen. Healing myself was my job. And the confrontation taught me that—by shocking me into reality. And despite my suffering during those three years afterward, I'm grateful for it all. Because, despite the pain—and there was a lot of it—I'm the better for it now. I'm a lot more mature and grown up. And a lot more resolved. It's actually been amazing."

Chapter 16: Confronting Parents, Part 2

Pete's confrontation of his mother reminds me of other parental confrontations I have heard of—and some that I have personally done. It's often a painful process, and, speaking for myself, the hopes and fantasies I personally held when I entered the confrontation rarely came true. But I always learned; from every confrontation I have always learned something, and sometimes *a lot*. And what I have learned consists primarily of two things: (1) more about the truth of my parents, and (2) more about the truth of myself.

I recall the last confrontation I had with my father, over the telephone around seven years ago. Not only did the confrontation fascinate me at the time, but it proved to be a turning point in our relationship—and in my relationship with myself. When I confronted him about his history of mistreating me—physically, verbally and of course emotionally—he became very defensive and started debating me by using the very defense attorney tactics I'd seen him use to great effect in the courtroom when I was a child. The difference, however, was that he was not defending some random criminal now: he was defending himself on charges of child abuse. And his accuser was his victim.

What struck me immediately was how brilliant he was. He was alternately slick, calm, intellectual, witty, aggressive, endearing, chummy, duplicitous and serious. When the subject of our discussion was less relevant he quickly sided with me compassionately, but when the subject grew serious he threw me to the wolves. I saw why he'd had a history of making good money and was popular among the criminal set. But his allies extended beyond their world. The judges liked him and sometimes had him over to their houses; sometimes I even went with him. The police liked him even though he sometimes made them look foolish. And the prosecutors liked him too, even though he had a good record of beating them. When I was a kid he loved telling and retelling the story about how he convinced a jury to find an accused murderer he defended not guilty, even though, wink-wink, everyone knew the guy had participated in the murder. He even wanted to write a book about this trial, with himself as the hero. He never got past the first few chapters, though, probably because the dishonesty of the story blunted his motivation.

Meanwhile, the first result of seeing my father's debate brilliance while I was confronting him was that I was flooded with empathy for my child self. No wonder I'd had to shut down emotionally and not fight back when I was a kid, 'his' kid: he was too smart and powerful for me. He was an unbeatable opponent. No child, especially a child under his dominion, could have beaten him.

But I was no longer that child and I believe that any objective jury of my peers would have agreed that I "won" in this confrontation. The reason I was able to defeat his brilliance was that I stuck with the truth, much as Pete did in his confrontation with his mother. The truth is a most powerful weapon. My father, like Pete's mother, was lying, or, to use the more psychologically polite phrase, was "in denial." And the more I prosecuted him the more his lies stood out starkly. And he knew it; I could feel it. There was a weird, unspoken subtext to our conversation. He wasn't used to losing against me. In fact, there was no precedent for it in our relational history. It humbled him, forcing him to reevaluate both me and himself. I realized that he wasn't used to pitting himself against a trained therapist with a younger mind who was also fighting for his life and had a lot more indicting evidence, that is, facts and truth. And also, I was a master at knowing my father's style, and that helped me. Some of the most powerful self-critical voices embedded in my head, the one's I've been struggling against for years, are his actual voice. So I've had practice debating him internally; years of it, in fact.

The end result of my confrontation of him was similar to the end result of Pete's, minus the terror of arrest: it shifted something within me, so much so that I didn't feel the need to go back to him again. It somehow freed me. I realized, strangely, that I'd won, not the debate so much, because that wasn't really important, but to me I'd won, to myself, some increased measure of my own self-respect. And inherent in that came more freedom for me. I say this with seven years' hindsight, but even at the time I felt it. Or felt something different, something within that had shifted.

Meanwhile, my father and I met a few times for lunch in the subsequent couple of years after that confrontation. It was strange to see him, because he treated me differently after that. He respected me more, though he never verbally admitted this nor admitted that I'd had any valid points in our "debate." But in a way I didn't care what he thought, because I knew what I thought. Somehow I wasn't chasing him or his opinion. This placed him in a position where he had to respect me more, because I respected myself more.

But even though over those lunches we spoke more like equals, he still occasionally reverted to type and tried to get in a dig at me by saying something insulting or offensive or ludicrous. But somehow I haven't had the urge to call him on his idiocy anymore—mostly because I'm not interested in being close with him. In that confrontation on the phone, he'd shown his hand of cards, I had shown mine and I just realized that confrontations would never go anywhere deeper or better with him.

And also, I would like to add this: I am glad that I confronted him over the telephone. At the time of that confrontation with him I was full of a lot of rage at him—in no small part because of the rage he'd expressed at me, through hitting me and the like—and the boundary of the telephone was probably very self-protective for me. I fear to think of the consequences had I hit him. It probably would have proven awful for me.

Meanwhile, in the last four or five years I haven't had any desire to see my father, mostly because he's not really that nice to me or interested in me, which is basically how he always was to me: neutral toward my existence, with occasional forays into the positive (if I played his game) and occasional forays into the negative (when I didn't). Nowadays he's become essentially irrelevant in my present-day life. And, to a pretty close degree, so too is my mother. I think that is one result of my ongoing self-therapy, as least as regards them. I have moved on, grown up and now don't really concern myself much with them. And weirdly, for the last year or so, to my surprise, I haven't found myself angry with them. When I first realized this, around the age of forty, I felt uncomfortable with it, almost like it was something shameful that I wasn't supposed to admit. For many years my anger toward my parents helped define my identity as an independent, free-thinking person. My anger operated as a sort of internal scaffolding that held my developing sense of self in place. My anger also operated to buttress my boundaries and in so doing helped me keep people from violating me. My anger was also a profound part of my healing process and was something always within reach. Without it I could easily become confused and really didn't know myself so well. I've thought about this a fair amount lately.

But the funny thing was, I hadn't even realized for a long time that my anger was slipping away, mostly because it wasn't slipping away: it was, I believe, simply working itself out. Untangling itself. I really didn't need it anymore. My assessment of what I'm going through is this: as the result of increasingly working through the grieving process I no longer am as traumatized as I was. Nothing will ever change what my parents did to me, but I feel that the wounds that resulted from what they did to me have, to a greater degree than ever before in my life, been healed. I admit that I remain suspicious of people who say they have recovered fully from their childhood trauma, because so many I know have said this and so few have demonstrated it to me. But still, I feel a lot of my work has paid off, even if I still have quite a ways yet to go.

Chapter 17: Confronting Parents, Part 3

I now wish to share more about others' experiences of confronting their parents. Confrontations fall on a variety of continuums. There are deep confrontations and shallow ones, intense confrontations and mild ones, lengthy ones and brief ones, direct ones and indirect ones, risky and safe ones and healthy ones and unhealthy ones.

The first confrontation I will share comes from a 60-year-old woman I met while traveling, Jill, who confronted her 85-year-old mother about having physically abused her when she was a girl.

"I had a lot of growing up to do before I confronted her," Jill told me. "And I'm glad I did, because I might have killed her if I'd confronted her earlier. I was that mad. I spent a lot of years fighting with my boyfriends and fighting in bars and beating the shit out of people, not realizing that I was really struggling to fight back against my old lady—and doing all the things to those folks that I secretly wanted to do to her. I'm lucky I didn't kill someone along the way, because if I had I wouldn't be sitting here telling you about it. I'd be rotting in some prison cell somewhere. And I'm also lucky someone didn't kill *me* along the way and, you know, I'm also lucky I didn't kill *myself*, what with all the drinking and drugging. But I eventually got wise, I started hanging around smarter people and I found I could actually face what she did to me and how it made me feel. It was then that I realized I needed to say something to her."

"How did it go?" I asked.

"Well," she replied, "I waited for the right time. I thought about it a lot and I talked it over with my boyfriend, a guy who's got some sense, and we came up with a decent plan. A few months back my mother needed me to help her winterize her house. It was a rush job because the frost came early, and we had to work together as a team—I'd do the work and she'd direct me. I realized this was my opportunity."

"So she was basically a captive audience?"

"Exactly," Jill said, nodding. "She couldn't escape, which is what she'd normally do. We had to finish the job that day."

"So what did you say to her?"

"Well, it was actually real simple. What I said was this: 'What did it sound like to you when I was a little girl and you were paddling my rear end and I was crying and screaming and coughing? What did that sound like to you?'"

"What did she reply?"

"I guess her reply wasn't too surprising. She said, 'I don't really remember thinking about it much.' Well, of course she didn't think about it much! Otherwise she wouldn't have done it!"

"How was that for you to hear?" I asked.

"Well, it's odd," Jill replied. "I mean, on one level it hurt, but on another level it was good—because I said it. Finally I spoke up for myself, even if it was fifty years later. And she knew exactly what I was getting at and she heard it. And she didn't deny that she paddled the piss out me. She just said that she 'didn't remember thinking about it much.' But I could tell by the tone in her voice that she knew what was what and that what she did was wrong. So she didn't deny it, and that was key. And by not denying it at some level she took responsibility for it."

"Did that change your relationship?" I asked.

"Yes," replied Jill firmly. "Yes it did. She respected me a lot more after that. She looked at me in a different way. Her eyes told me that. She knew that I knew, that I hadn't forgotten. And she knew that back when she was beating my backside blue there was a real person there, crying. She was beating a real human being and now that human being was back to let her know how it felt. And it did *not* feel good."

A lesson I draw from Jill's confrontation is that when people are older and actually want to maintain a relationship with their parents, the confrontations tend to go more smoothly. For instance, Jill did not want to break from her mother: she wanted to insert a new perspective on reality into their relationship by standing up for the child she once was. I think I, on the other hand, was desirous to break up with my father, even if I still held some secret hope that he might change and love me and grow as the result of the confrontation. The same goes for Pete: although he might have had some hope of sparking some remnant of love in his mother, he'd raised the bar pretty high for her and was treating the confrontation as a last-ditch effort for them to have a serious, intimate relationship. Also, he was willing to walk away from their relationship if she couldn't rise to the occasion. But in Jill's case, she actually demanded little of her mother past asking her a simple question. And she also did it in the context of providing her mother a needed service, so that her mother was, to some degree, obligated to maintain civility and remain open.

A very different type of confrontation, both riskier and more intense, involves those who try to bring a sexually abusive parent to justice by taking steps to have him arrested for his crimes. These confrontations can go in several directions. I have known a couple of people who confronted their fathers from the witness stand at the trial. One was Stanley, age 34, whose father had abused him when he was a teenager.

"Even though the jury ultimately found him not guilty," said Stanley, "I think over time I benefitted from the experience of the trial anyway—or found ways to benefit. But this is looking back on it all with twelve years of hindsight. I don't mean to minimize the horror of what that trial did to me, because it really messed me up—those mercenary lawyers and all the lies and bullshit being spread by them and the experts they hired. For about five years I regretted pressing charges; I think I went in with too much fantasy—that I would simply have my say and everyone would just see the obvious about what kind of man he was. And that's not how it went, though I did get to confront him—and say the things I'd always wanted to say. But it came at a big cost. It really fucked with my head at the time and for a while afterwards. It shattered my self-confidence. I had to dig myself out, from the bottom up. But I will say this: for a few hours I did have the satisfaction of seeing that slimeball in the hot seat. He had fear in his eyes. Real fear. And I could tell that he thought, for a while, when I was testifying, that people, the judge and the jury and the people in the audience, might just believe the truth, at which point he'd be going away for a long, long time—to a not very nice place where people don't take kindly to men who molest their sons. He was afraid. And I never saw him afraid when I was a child, not one time—and I'll probably never see it again. His fear when I was telling what he did to me and how it made me feel was the closest thing I'll ever get to an admission from him. I've thought about his look a lot—and I still get satisfaction from it. It's helped my healing process in some very important ways. I'll never forget that look. It actually gave me the cornerstone for rebuilding my confidence."

But not everyone felt so empowered throughout this process.

"I tried to get my father arrested for raping me," said Kelley, a 27-year-old woman who had just started college after struggling for years to get her life on track. "But the whole thing backfired on me. Hardly anyone took me seriously—because I had convictions for prostitution and drug possession on my record and because I got put in a psych ward when I was seventeen. They felt I wasn't 'reliable' enough, that my word was shit. And all I really wanted was to tell the world what my father did to me. I wanted to stare him in the face and let him know that the reason my life went totally off the rails was because of him. Not because I had some stupid chemical imbalance like the shrinks said or a 'disease of drug addiction' like they tried to ram down my throat in rehab. Fuck that. All those nights when I was a kid, him slipping in my room—and my mom pretending she didn't know. *They* messed me up. It would have messed anyone up. I actually wanted to blast both of them—publicly—with both barrels. I even had fantasies of having her arrested too—watching her squirm just like I used to. She knew he was a pervert and she didn't do shit. But I figured out pretty quick, when I was 22, that if they wouldn't even arrest him, and he was a straight-up rapist, then they certainly weren't going to go after her. It was all just a punch in the guts. My life fell apart even worse after that. More drugs, and all that went with it—more sex, more treating myself like I was worthless. I was so lost and needed to numb out my feelings."

"So trying to get him arrested wasn't worth it?" I asked.

"No," she said, "it wasn't. But at the same time, yes, looking back on it five years later, I can say that it was—in a strange way. What I've come to realize now is that taking the stand I took, even if it didn't come to shit legally, wasn't all bad. I think some part of me still emerged the better for trying to have that man arrested. *I* took the action. *I* made the decision. *I* did my part. *I* walked into that police station on my own—me, with my legal record and my tattoos—and *I* gave a full statement. *I* stood up to my father. I'm proud of what I did. And even if he and my mom weren't there to hear it, *I* confronted that prick out loud with a cop in a uniform at a desk in a private room listening to me and writing down every word, including my father's full name and date of birth. And that, in its own little tiny way, did give me some boost of strength. It's not my fault the legal system was so full of cowards. It's not my fault my dad holds a normal job and puts on a tie in the morning and is a supposedly respected citizen. *I* tried. *I* defended myself. And I feel brave for what I did—I *was* brave. And as time goes on I respect myself more and more for what I did, even if the world at the time couldn't stand by me."

"Hmm," I said. "Not simple stuff."

"No," replied Kelley. "Not simple at all. I don't know that I'd recommend anyone trying what I tried. I've actually talked with a couple of women—and one guy even, a gay friend of mine—who tried what I tried and just got turned away by the cops and the district attorney, just like I did. Flimsy excuses, always. It's fucked up. But in the end I think I'm glad I did it, even though when they decided not to go forward with prosecuting him it felt like I was getting raped all over again—by *them* this time. It was not good. I feel like I'm just coming out of it now. Five years later."

Yet sometimes the legal system does work more clearly to someone's advantage in confronting an abusive parent. Occasionally I have heard of people who got one of their abusers convicted.

"My father got sentenced to prison for nine years," said Heather, a young woman I met whose father had forced her to have oral sex on him when she was a child. "He's done three of those years already."

"How did you feel when they found him guilty?" I asked her.

"Relieved," she replied. "Relieved and yet, somehow—and this surprised me—ambivalent. The process of going through the trial was hell, and frankly for most of it I thought I was going to lose, especially when my dad's lawyer was trying to prove I was delusional—which is the same shit my dad *and* my mom always told me when I was a kid. But in the end—and I still find this amazing—the jury saw through his dishonesty and realized that I was legit, that I was telling the whole truth and nothing but the truth. It also helped that he'd done stuff to other girls, and they let that be entered as evidence, so my words were in a way corroborated. But still—I still thought of him as all-powerful, invincible...that I could never affect him. That he made the rules and that was the end of the story. So it was the weirdest feeling when they said 'guilty' and led him out in handcuffs. And he just looked like this crumpled up, little, middle-aged man—done for. I just couldn't believe it. Some group of average people had finally believed me—and announced it publicly. It felt like I was tripping on acid. But I hadn't even had a cup of coffee that day. In some ways I still don't know what to make of it."

"So that was the ambivalence?" I asked.

"Yes," Heather replied. "That and more. I had flashbacks throughout the trial and afterward too—and nightmares. Ones in which they found him not guilty. Ones in which I was the one on trial. And ones in which he was abusing me all over again—to punish me for trying to bring him to justice. In my family, after all, I was the criminal for speaking up—and for bringing in outsiders to protect me. I even felt guilty about that in some of the nightmares, and when I woke up too. That's how confused I was by all of it—by the 'fair' trial where he got to have *his* say and take his best shot at proving that I was a liar and a nutcase. I've also had a few nightmares since the trial in which I stood up in front of the whole courtroom and publicly admitted I *had* lied. What the fuck was that? It was crazy—those dreams. I'd wake up paralyzed—even suicidal. Totally insane. Tears all over my face and pillow, and sweating buckets. I think I was just terrified. Flooded with everything that had happened and was happening. Like some part of him still had some big old chunk of control over me. I really had to talk myself down. It took everything I had—plus a lot of help from my friends, and even from my dog Charlie. And yet, in spite of all the bad stuff, I got a new memory from it all—I *have* a new memory, a totally true memory—of something different: of them leading him, my father, out in handcuffs at the end of the trial, of him being so docile and obedient—and small. It brings me back to reality. And I remember just sitting there in the courtroom chair crying—and crying and crying. I somehow knew that I'd told the truth and the world had heard. It was a relief. It didn't make up for what he did to me, it didn't make up for the flashbacks and the nightmares, but it did help. Somehow. I confronted my worst perpetrator. I guess I just figure there was no way for me to confront him without it being at least a little ugly for me. Those ugly consequences were bound to come."

Meanwhile, confrontations of parents can take ugly turns in different ways, especially if the intensity gets ramped up too high in an unsafe environment. I recently heard the following story from a young man I met in California, Edward, who verbally confronted both his parents about his father having whipped him as a child and about his mother having not just stood by and watched but having regularly provoked his father to do it. During the confrontation, which became heated when his father started screaming at Edward and labeled him a "liar" and a "pansy" and a "wimp," his father, who was no longer young, began having heart palpitations. At this point Edward's mother called 911 for an ambulance and had her husband rushed to the hospital. She then told Edward, the ambulance drivers and the emergency room doctor, not to mention the entire extended family, that she blamed Edward for his father's problems. And ultimately she and Edward's father cut Edward from their will.

"Was the confrontation worth it?" I asked.

"No," he said. "No. I lost more than I gained. It really messed me up."

"But you gained something?"

"Yes," he replied, "I did. Oddly enough, I gained awareness of how awful my parents are. The confrontation caused them to take off their mask and show me the wolves they really are, even if they see themselves as good Christian sheep. Maybe that information will become valuable to me someday, but right now it just feels awful. I was hoping, which probably means that I'm psychotic, that my parents would admit stuff and welcome me back into the family with open arms. Instead I only got myself thrown out. It stinks. And my brother and my sister are both laughing at me, all the way to the bank. But I guess life throws us a curveball once in a while. Live and learn. But sometimes it's fucking rotten."

I also heard a similar story from a young woman in Massachusetts, Susan, who verbally confronted her mother for having repeatedly "mind-fucked" her. Susan read pages of her journal to her mostly silent mother, pages of detailed memories and feelings and reflections. Her mother's reaction was to attempt suicide that night by overdosing on pills.

The family sided with the mother against Susan.

Afterward, they said: "You tried to kill your mother! Are you happy now?"

Susan herself felt suicidal after that and only felt her suicidal feelings abate when she apologized to her mother. It was some years later, which is when I met Susan, did she realize that the confrontation had only resulted in her feeling "mind-fucked" by her mother yet again.

"When I figured that out," Susan told me, "I didn't become suicidal: I became enraged. But now at least I'm smart enough to stay away from that wicked witch. I'm never going back to her or my father or my sisters and their husbands. And I won't confront my mother again. No way."

"Why not?" I asked.

"She'd only crucify me if I confronted her," replied Susan. "Hell, she'd crucify me no matter what I do, so I might as well stay away from her and enjoy my life as best I can. I guess I had to learn that lesson through confronting her, though. I'm just lucky I made it out alive!"

I will now share a different sort of confrontation that struck me as effective. William is a 44-year-old man I met at one of my film screenings. He wanted to tell me about confronting his parents. They'd made him into the family scapegoat when he was little, humiliating him to the degree of sorely crushing his self-esteem. He said that he first went to therapy to deal with his rage at them.

"It was in therapy that I first made up my mind to confront those two beasts," he said, "I wanted to march right over to their house and burn it down with them inside. But my shrink had the sense to talk me off the ledge. She said, 'William, it's not worth spending your life in prison over them: hasn't forty years of emotional prison been long enough?' Well, you know what, she was right. Goddammit, she was right. It was like a lightbulb that went on for me."

"Yet did you confront them?" I asked.

"Hell yeah," he replied. "But actually confronting them was the last stage. Before that my shrink actually helped me a lot here. First, though, she and I spent about a year confronting the parts of *me* that were just *like* my parents."

"You mean the parts of them they'd put in your head?"

"Exactly. Before my shrink brought it up I never even knew they were there. She really helped me see that. And that was hard as shit to do—and helped me realize that I was jumping the gun by wanting to confront my actual parents in person. There was no way they would be able to hear what I was saying if I myself, *with* a therapist's help, couldn't even see how I was just *like* them! So instead, during that year of therapy, I cut them off. That was the second thing. No contact whatsoever. Cold turkey. Fuck off, assholes! And that in itself was a sort of confrontation, but not a direct one. But they got the message loud and clear. Little William who accepted the blame for everything wasn't taking their crap anymore. Game the fuck over."

"Did they try to contact you?"

"Oh, hell yeah, constantly. They tried everything: pity, rage, humiliation, insults, guilt trips, fake kindness, birthday presents, money, using my nasty brothers as go-betweens, emails, phone calls, notes tacked to the windshield of my car. Hell, if they thought it would have worked, they would have tried skywriting from an airplane. It was actually very interesting to watch. They were like chickens running around with their heads cut off, real sickos. I had no idea they'd go to the lengths they went to suck me back into their clan. I guess at some level I was pretty important to them, in a sick way, that is. But anyway, I never responded. I just brought it in to therapy and discussed it and also wrote about it too on my own, in my journal. I'm not much good at writing journals and my spelling sucks but I get the point across and I save everything I write. So anyway, for the first time in my life I started feeling like an adult. And I also realized what wounded little kids they were. They were behaving like out-of-control kids on the playground. Dangerous kids, but kids."

"But eventually you did confront them?" I asked.

"Yes," he replied, "once I felt strong and secure enough, like I was enough of my own ally."

"In person?"

"No," replied William. "Hell no. That was too risky, in every way. I did it with email. Calmly, rationally and very carefully. I wrote a few drafts of the letter before I sent it and I shared each draft with my shrink. We talked about my motives and my goals and we went at a really slow pace. I took out all the threats, all the bitter emotion, and just wrote exactly what I wanted to say: what they did to me and exactly how it made me feel. I also explained why I was done being a part of their lives."

"Did they reply?" I asked.

"Of course they did," he said. "With all their usual nonsense. More rage, denials, threats, blame, ganging up, twisting facts, belittling me, accusations, self-pity, complete lack of responsibility, begging, pleading— their same old bag of tricks. They're like human glue traps and they still think I'm a mouse, dumb enough to walk into anything. But I'm not a mouse anymore."

"So they didn't trap you?"

"Nope," he replied with a smile. "No they did not. Instead I printed out their replies and shared them with my therapist and also analyzed them in my journal. It really was quite enlightening and it grew me up a lot. It also helped that I kept a copy of the letter I wrote them, because if you heard their side of it you'd think I wrote a completely different letter. But that was the story of my life; I never got to be who I really was. I was always made into some monster or half-human creature. So the confrontation entered some familiar territory. It was like revisiting the worst of my childhood, but with a real adult ally on my side."

"The ally being your therapist?"

"No," he laughed. "I actually meant myself! That's been the benefit of all this. I finally became an adult. I actually quit therapy shortly after that. I realized I could take care of this stuff on my own. I grew up, or at least I realized I could take care of my own growing up on my own. And my therapist acknowledged it. She was pretty good, that shrink. Dressed like shit but she *saved* my goddamn life!"

The last story of a confrontation I would like to share is different from the others. I heard it from Gregory, age 26, who was raised by a single mother. Gregory found me through one of my internet videos on confronting parents and wanted to share his story with me. His mother, a travel agent, had had a sort of breakdown—an 'existential crisis,' in her words—when Gregory was a year old. For six months she'd gone to live on an ashram in India, during which time she'd placed him in the care of an uncle and aunt. This had traumatized Gregory and left him with a multitude of issues around abandonment. Gregory recently spoke with me about confronting her over this.

"So at first she got all defensive," Gregory said. "I confronted her out of the blue—didn't even warn her I was planning it or give it any context. I started accusing her at the dining room table one morning when I was home from college on vacation and she was getting ready to leave for work. She just turtled up—closed up shop emotionally—and was useless in the interaction. I tried that way a few more times—because I think *I* felt safer when she was caught off-guard—but it never went anywhere. Finally she actually took the lead and said that maybe we could set aside a proper time and space to discuss it."

"And you agreed?" I asked.

"Yeah," he replied. "I decided it was worth it. I talked about it a lot with my friends, and I'd been reading a lot of psychology, and I felt I'd give her a fair deal in speaking on her own behalf, especially when I considered that when I caught her off-guard nothing useful came of it."

"So what happened?"

"Well, actually it sparked some really good conversation—mostly because she actually agreed with most of my points. I was surprised how insightful and sophisticated she was."

"Hmm," I said. "That's not always so common."

"No, I would imagine it isn't," he replied. "And I wasn't expecting it. But one thing we talked about—and we've talked about it a lot since—is that she's actually wanted to talk about some of this stuff with me for a long time but didn't know how. Yet when I brought it up without any warning she couldn't handle it."

"So can you tell me more," I asked, "about what happened in the confrontation, and as the result of it? I'm curious."

"Sure," Gregory replied. "She talked a lot about her own childhood and why she had her crisis or breakdown or whatever it was, and how painful it must have been for me when I was a little boy. We both were able to share on a really deep emotional level about this — in a lot of detail. And I really appreciate that. In many ways we see things the same way."

"So it was cool?"

"Yeah...yes...in some ways. But in some ways not. In some ways I actually feel kind of confused about it still. Like, one thing she makes clear over and over is that she can't change the past. She wishes it had been different, but there's nothing she can do except acknowledge it fully and be there for me as much as can be reasonably expected given my age and level of independence. And in a way that sounds fair to me."

"Okay," I said. "Makes sense. But can you describe how exactly that is confusing?"

"Well," he replied, "it's confusing for a few reasons. One is that I feel it's a little too easy for her to say 'it's all done, it's in the past, and I can't change it. I can only change the here and now.' Even though that might seem reasonable I still feel it's a sort of a cop-out, because I'm not really sure that she's doing *everything* she can to change her life now—or that she really fully acknowledges what she did to me then. I mean, for starters she never takes responsibility for having gotten pregnant by my loser dad —though that's a separate issue. I'd like to confront him too but I don't even know where to find him. But her abandonment of me—I think it still overwhelms her. Actually I haven't thought about this so fully. But this is what I'm feeling now."

"Interesting," I said.

"Yeah—it is actually interesting. And feels safe for me to talk about. The thing that gets me is one thing my mother said—and I don't like to repeat it, but it nags at me. It's that she feels that her having had me, her having given birth to me and having been so deeply attached to me, gave her the safety and the security to really be able to do the deep healing that *she* needed to do—because she, in her words, 'owed me that.' And she feels that part of her owing me a better mother, a mother who could heal from her own ghastly childhood, was that she needed to have her breakdown, or whatever you call it, so she could eventually have a 'breakthrough' and become a more whole person. And it almost sounds like she's proud when she talks about this, like what she did was a good thing, and she gets defensive when I express anger at her for abandoning me, like somehow I'm raining on her healing parade. So in a way it's like she's blaming me for being pissed off at her for having her existential breakdown, like somehow this is my fault. Like I need to let go of it or thank her or something. Hmm...this is confusing to describe."

"No," I said. "I think I'm following you pretty well. And I think it goes deeper than how she's looking at this. Like she doesn't fully see things through your lens, the lens of your childhood experience."

"Yes!" said Gregory. "Exactly. It does feel that way. It really does. The thing that I keep coming back to in my head, which I tried to say to her but she didn't really seem able to hear, is that she seemed to be using *me* to do her healing—and yet she said she was doing her healing *for my sake*. Like at some fundamental level in her mind she feels that justifies her abandoning me, even if she says she feels bad about it. And maybe at one level she *was* healing for my sake, somehow, and I guess I should be grateful for that, but at another level there's a big part of me that feels she should have done all that healing, had that breakdown and breakthrough and done all that other shit, *before she had me*, and just left me out of her mess: not put any of the responsibility of her cracking up and going to India on me, not do it for my sake, not make me suffer the consequences of it. After all, I had no desire to have a screwed up, depressed mother who went mental and gave me away to a bunch of biologically-related strangers and then took me back when she was feeling better. I needed a mom there for me—not a mom sorting through her own miserable childhood while I was actually living my real childhood."

"Did you share any of this with her?"

"Yes. In a way I did. I have. But like I said, she doesn't really seem to get it. It's like she's missing some piece of herself that is able to understand me. It's like, when it gets down to the core of the onion she just sides with her own wounded child before mine—every time. It's like she seems to think that at some inherent level I should just be grateful to her for giving me life, and that that has given her a *carte blanche* to have had her breakdown. Like she really feels blameless in some place inside herself where she's never taken responsibility. And I feel that to her, in that place, I just don't count. Like my feelings don't count. And my deeper gut vibe is that my feelings, at that level, never did count to her. If I had counted she wouldn't have left for India, no matter what. I was just an object to her, not a subject. I was an object there for her to use, but not one that was as important to her as she was to herself. And while I don't feel it's her job to mother me anymore, because I'm an adult, there's some part of me that doesn't love her and probably never will, especially if she can't acknowledge this reality within herself and within our relationship. It's really like we cannot connect in that basic place—like she really can't acknowledge some basic things or take responsibility for some basic things. She can't go there. Like she's genuinely blocked. It's like we're really different beings. Like there's some connection of consciousness that's just missing in her."

"How has this affected your relationship with her?"

"It's weird," he replied, "because I really am confused. I mean, in some ways the fact that she's acknowledged so much more than I ever expected has brought us closer and made me feel so much more loving toward her and less angry, but at the same time, when I hit that barrier inside her and see how deeply defensive she is about some of that basic stuff, I realize I can't be that close with her. I figured this out a while ago. And I realized I had to get away. I don't know for how long, but I had to leave and take distance. I actually haven't spent that much time with her in a while. And when I got the chance to take a job in Oregon—and she lives in Georgia—I took it. I moved away. And somehow it's felt better. The distance helps. It brings me clarity. And I need it."

Chapter 18: Working in the World

Many of us who break from our parents find it difficult to fit into society. We put so much energy into dismantling the templates of our past that it can be disorienting to enter a world that strongly upholds our parents' values and patterns. This can sap the very energy we prefer to spend on inner healing. Yet the conundrum is that we owe it to ourselves to be independent adults, which means living and functioning *in* society. If we never manage to function as adults then essentially the sick sides of our parents win: they have rendered us permanent children. And so we must take the action of working in the world.

Often we are pressured to put energy into being able to interact with, and interact comfortably with, people who hold values that oppose ours. Often we are expected to slide through their world of dissociation and function in spite of it—and attain financial independence while playing by the rules of their game. Some people who take strides to break from their parents are better at this than others. They manage to find more or less stable employment that satisfies them and sometimes even enhances their growth. It helps if they have good-enough boundaries to be able to interface with people radically less healthy than themselves without becoming triggered. This is not easy and for many people it takes years, if not decades, to achieve.

I would like to share the history of my process of becoming a more functionally independent adult in the world. Although I had many years of struggling to fit into society, I have also had some good working years, especially most recently. I feel fortunate that my path has flowered. For instance, I was able to use my life experience and my education to become a psychotherapist. This work, which I did for a decade, allowed my whole life to revolve around the most important thing to me: healing. I lived and breathed healing and also lived and breathed studying the defenses, my own and others', that resist healing. And I treasured it; it was useful to others and it provoked my own growth and learning. And now it has led me to my newest career: that of a documentary filmmaker.

But it took me a long time to build up to this and some of the years before I became a therapist were rough. I worked as a restaurant waiter, I worked as an office secretary, I did manual labor, I performed music at children's birthday parties, I did proofreading, I cooked pizza, I worked as a camp counselor and I washed dishes. And sometimes I was unemployed and under a lot of stress. Not infrequently I was jealous of my "normal" friends—those who were happily building careers and finding romantic partners and preparing for having kids and saving money and not seeming so lost or tortured over the nature of their existence. Part of me wanted to be like them. And part of me knew that I needed to figure how to fake being like them if I wanted to survive. I filled out job applications, I went to interviews with employers who sometimes saw me as odd, I tried my best to squeeze my personality into an employable little box of normalcy and I spent endless hours waiting fruitlessly for their return phone calls.

And for a while my battle seemed like a losing cause: for two years, when I was 24 and 25, I ran out of inspiration and moved in with my mother and slept on her couch. I became a sort of hermit, living miserably on the edge of society. I all but gave up trying to find work and instead practiced guitar, wrote three travelogues that never got published, paid no rent and did a lot of journaling. My mother became my closest companion and I became almost like her live-in emotional boyfriend. I don't enjoy recalling that time. Those were the two most depressing years of my adult life, by far. I grew a scraggly beard, had hardly any friends, sporadically wore deodorant and had no good idea of how to pull myself out of the rut into which I'd fallen. I was lost and often retreated into a fantasy that somehow it was the world's responsibility, and not mine, to save me. And when that clearly didn't happen I found myself repeating a despairing, self-pitying monologue that went something like this: "Oh world, why don't you see my value? You should respect me, not ignore me! You should be banging on my door to hire me! It's you that is the problem, not me!"

I was missing the point. Although our world was and is screwed up, the bigger issue as regards breaking from my parents and becoming my own independent person was that I had failed in some basic ways to live up to my responsibility to take care of myself. This was based on some of my troubled early childhood templates that I couldn't yet accept: that despite the fact that my parents had not fully done their jobs in helping me develop an independent internal and external identity, now that I was an adult the world owed me nothing. I had to grow up.

Yet I know others who are breaking from their families who have gotten more stuck than I did. I think of George, a 46-year-old artist and internet acquaintance of mine who has received government psychiatric disability for most of his adult life. Although in one sense he has permanently broken away from his parents, because he has no contact with them and largely understands the ways in which they crippled him, on another level he hasn't broken from them at all and remains crippled, because he has transferred his unrecovered feelings of dependency from them onto the government. The irony is that he, like many people on disability that I know, hates the government and rails against it at the first chance he gets, even though they pay his rent, his food and his transportation. It's a safe way to hate his parents by proxy—and to avoid having to take adult responsibility for himself.

Or I think of Patricia. She broke contact with her parents only to get into an emotionally dead marriage and then to have three children with her husband.

"I'm trapped," she emailed me. "I stay home with my kids all day long, I have no room to be creative, I'm mostly bored and I can't leave my husband. And I can't even work because I wouldn't be able to make enough money to pay for the kids' daycare. I know this is not my kids' fault and that I should have figured this out before I got married and pregnant, but basically I screwed myself. I thought I was so liberated by cutting off my parents, yet here I am even less liberated than my mother was. I actually receive Food Stamps now. I hate using them, but I need to. My husband doesn't make enough to support us."

In this vein, many courageous people I know broke with their parents at great emotional risk only to find that there was little positive waiting for them after the break. There was no reward, no laughter, no love and no party. Instead there was sometimes silence, sometimes lack of any interaction at all and almost always a lot of jumbled, intense and painful feelings to process.

Thomas, a friend of mine who's a 58-year-old interior designer, says, "It was dreadful when I broke away from my parents. I was 23 and really in a bad way — so lost and confused and financially broke on top of it. I had a spiffy college degree in business, but I wasn't emotionally in a position to go out and land a decent job. I could barely force myself to brush my teeth or take a shower. All I could do was walk and meditate. Finally, though, the clouds parted when I joined a free therapeutic study group. Somehow that gave me the strength to just swallow my pride and get a job that complemented my inner world."

"What kind of work did you do?"

"I cleaned people's apartments. My first clients were a few people in my therapy group. Then later I also worked as the caretaker of a local community center — which allowed me to get health insurance. I ended up doing this for more than twenty years. At first I was a bit ashamed by it, that basically I was a janitor and a house cleaner, me with my fancy business degree, but once I was able to acknowledge to myself that I was doing it to save my own life—on a deep psychological level, which basically no one else I knew was doing—I accepted the work and respected myself for it. And I grew up. And what's funny is once the results of my growing up started to show, people respected me too. Everyone did. Eventually, when I really got my emotional life in order, I went back to night school for interior design and then really came into my own in a profession that suited me. And all those people I cleaned for suddenly started referring me clients for my new business. Rich people too! It really shocked me, in a way. And I did all this without family support."

"So you never took money from your family?" I asked.

"Never," he replied. "After college, not a nickel. Somehow I knew that achieving my own financial independence was part of my ticket to psychological freedom. And what's funny is that my two brothers both had better jobs than I did but were always whining to my parents for money. Beggars, they were. They always needed more. Where's the self-respect in that? They never broke away and they never emotionally grew up. And my parents loved them for it. Me, I broke away. I cut the financial apron strings and at some level declared my independence. I had to sacrifice for my choices, because I traveled a tough, creative path on so many levels, but the end result of my path was that I got *me*."

"In some ways your story reminds me of mine," I said, "except for those two years I lived with my mother. Somehow, by being so close to her, I lost my fight. I lost some important part of my passion, even if I did become a much better guitar player and writer during that time. You know, I actually only moved out of my mother's place because she met a guy she wanted to marry. She no longer wanted me around so she booted me out. That was terrifying for me, because I'd grown socially weak in those two years. I actually resented her for throwing me out, but I luckily managed to avoid getting stuck in resentment and instead to land on my feet."

"You went to work?" Thomas asked.

"Yes," I replied. "I did. I had to. And while the first jobs I got after not working for two years were rather mindless and were certainly low-paying, they saved my life. I mostly did data entry, because I had learned to type so quickly from all that journaling. Eventually, though, I got better jobs, ones that gave me more independence, more time and more freedom. And eventually I went back to grad school to become a therapist. I took out loans and paid for it myself. Actually, though, when I think back on it, my grandmother did send me a check for five thousand dollars for school. That was generous of her, and it helped, because grad school was expensive—about forty thousand dollars."

"Good for her," said Thomas. "And good for you for accepting it."

"Yeah," I replied, "I think you're right. I admit, I considered ripping up the check and sending it back, because my grandmother was so intensely on my mother's side, but on the other hand, I was glad for the money. And I'm glad I took it. It helped. She did me a good turn there. And certainly none of my other cousins—her other grandchildren—turned down her money, and I know she gave some of them a lot more than she gave me. She told me that! But still, she did help me when I needed it, and I'm glad for that."

This reminds me of the story of Roxanne, an acquaintance in her mid-twenties who broke contact with her parents five years earlier, while she was halfway through college. Both of her parents had behaved cruelly toward her when she was little, and even though Roxanne felt that they treated her well in other ways she realized that keeping in contact with them was suffocating her spirit. But she was terrified to break away from them for fear that they would stop paying for her tuition and university housing.

"But eventually," Roxanne said, "I realized I needed to break up with them at all costs: even at the cost of having to drop out of school. At that point I wrote them a confronting letter. I explained exactly why I no longer wanted anything to do with them and I said it in no uncertain terms. I was so scared! But I needed to say it, for my own growth and self-respect. It was a defining moment of my life."

"How did you handle the issue of money?" I asked.

"That was what terrified me the worst," she replied. "Or at least that's what I focused on in my obsessions—and that's what kept popping up in my nightmares. I can't tell you how many times I woke up freaked out and short of breath—in a panic attack. But here's how I handled it: I said nothing. I figured they knew I needed the money and that the question of money was implicit. I didn't want to beg and I figured if they were halfway decent people they would do the right thing."

"And did they?" I asked.

"Oddly enough, they did. They didn't cut me off. And you know, I really respect them for it. They did write me back and say that they felt very hurt by my decision and that they didn't understand it—which is typical of them, because they don't want to understand it—but they said that they didn't want to punish me for it and that they would continue to pay for my university."

"Wow," I said. "Kudos to them."

"Yep," Roxanne confirmed. "True. At first, though, I was suspicious that they were secretly trying to guilt-trip me, because they did that so much when I was a kid. But I decided to take their words at face value. I decided not to do what I'd always done—giving in to my guilt—and instead I just kept going to school and doing my thing."

"Did you reply to their letter?"

"I did," she replied. "Just once. I said, 'I understand and I thank you for continuing to pay for my education.' They wrote me back a lot more after that and left endless messages on my voice mail, but I didn't reply, at least for a couple of years. Meanwhile, I finished school and then got a job and I've been working every since. So I never needed their money after that."

"Did they ever offer you more?" I asked.

"Yes," she said. "Strangely enough, they did offer me more. But I refused. I wanted to be free. I actually hated it that they were paying for my education, but I really didn't have much choice there. Plus, in a way I felt like it was still okay to be a kid when I was in college. But after that, it was game over: time to grow up!"

"And how has it been since then?" I asked.

"Much better," she said. "I'm completely self-supporting and on my own. And that feels great. I mean, sometimes I do admit to feeling jealous when I see my friends getting really nice gifts from their parents, like a new computer or help with their rent so that they can live in a better neighborhood. And I know my sister gets those kinds of gifts from my parents too—a new laptop, a free vacation with her boyfriend, et cetera. But for me, when I think of the cost of accepting my parents' money nowadays, I shudder. I totally prefer going through life on my own. I like being a real adult. I've actually never been happier."

"But did you ever feel like a hypocrite," I asked, "accepting their money after you broke up with them? I know that sometimes I did."

"Funny that you ask that," she replied. "I did and I didn't. I definitely felt weird about it. And some of my friends sort of called me a hypocrite. But I realized I really wasn't. I really felt that my parents had a responsibility to help me get my needed education. But what really cleared up the hypocrisy question for me was when I realized that if I had kids and they cut me off I'd still pay for their education. And I'd still love them. I knew that. And so I accepted my parents' money, without guilt."

SECTION 3: TOWARD A NEW LIFE

Chapter 19: Guilt and the Holidays

Holidays can be a painful and triggering time for people breaking from their parents. Most holidays celebrate the family and offer little encouragement to people who explore the opposite. I cannot tell you the number of times I have heard people of the norm say to me: "What? You're not spending Christmas with your parents? That must be so sad for them!"

I used to feel defensive when I heard that. In recent years, however, when I hear such a comment I usually ignore it, even though it still stings to have people who don't even know my family instinctively and unconsciously side with my parents. But is it worth arguing with people about this? Usually not, unless I find the speaker worth engaging, which doesn't happen too often. But if I do find the speaker worth it, I instead reply bluntly.

"Yes, it *is* sad for them," I might say, "because they are deprived of the person to whom they were addicted to taking advantage of. But it's actually no longer really sad *for me*. It's actually a major relief for me. I no longer have to feel pressure to play their emotional games, to feel sickened observing their dynamics, to put up with their digs and rude questions, to feel guilty standing up for myself, to feel emotionally hungover for days afterward, not to mention to have to shut down emotionally beforehand in preparation. Life is better now. Now I spend my holidays around people I prefer. Or I can be alone—with my own loving self. Either way, now I get to be around people who treat me well and I get to do fun things. Holidays now are more often than not relaxing, and really *are* a holiday, not all the emotional buildup and inevitable letdown that I got taught again and again as a kid."

But it's taken me a lot of years to get to this point. Coming out of the trance the family had put me in was a long, slow, often unpleasant and often scary process.

In 1999, when I was 27, I first avoided my family for the holiday season — which for me was Thanksgiving, Christmas and New Year's. I had only recently taken major distance from them and was in the process of reformulating my conception of myself — who I was, how I fit into the world, who my important social relationships were, what I held to be true and what my obligation to others were. The holiday season ramped up the intensity of my inner process to a painful degree. It wasn't fun.

I best remember that Thanksgiving. I spent it with my new best friend and we had been invited to one of his friend's homes for the all-American Thanksgiving dinner. Many others had also been invited and there was a great layout of food, a din of good conversation and even some singing. I participated as best I could, but my heart was heavy with emotional pain. I felt plagued with thoughts about my family. In a way I felt I really missed them, but it wasn't exactly that: it was guilt, guilt for depriving *them* of my presence, guilt for throwing a wrench into their works. I knew that they, especially my mother, felt awful that I was avoiding her on the holiday. But was I really guilty?

As a child, my parents trained me, according to parental privilege, to prioritize feeling *their* feelings over feeling my own. I felt their sadness, their anger, their fear, their frustration and their anxiety. I was, however, fully allowed to feel all my own reactive feelings, like guilt or shame. Also, my parents trained me to feel that I had no right to avoid being in their home on the holidays. And they created a family narrative to justify their logic. They trained me to remember only the happy times, the happy Christmas moments, the happy holiday meals, the lovely holiday photos, the snow in the backyard and the lovely music playing and the pumpkin pie with sugary whipped cream. And to one degree or other these memories were all true. They also trained me to be excited and hopeful for the coming holidays and to feel only love and warmth for my family. And they also trained me to push away my painful memories. Those were the ones we never spoke about, such that according to family lore they didn't exist.

They trained me with a wall of silence to forget those childhood times when I as an early teenager had supposedly "misbehaved" at the dinner table and my father, with a red face, purple neck veins and bulging neck muscles, had slapped me in the face, called me awful names, physically dragged me out of the house and locked me out on the cold back porch of our Upstate New York home in my socks while the rest of my family, with not a word spoken, ate their supper "in peace." They also trained me to forget that no one but my father, who took about fifteen or twenty minutes to calm down, came out to "fetch me" back in, not even my supposedly "protective mother bear" of a mother, even though I'd really done nothing wrong and my father had only attacked me because I was a convenient target for him to blow off his steam from a frustrating day in court as a lawyer.

They also trained me to forget that one Thanksgiving, only a dozen years before 1999, when my father had gone into a rage attack at the dinner table because my mother had secretly gotten drunk earlier in the afternoon. They trained me to forget him smacking a wine glass into the wall, to forget the glass exploding everywhere and to forget one of my young relatives who was present screaming in pain when some of the stinging wine went into her eyes. They trained me also to forget my mother, with her slurred voice, cleaning it all up, saying everything was "okay now, it's all okay now," my father apologizing and all of us going back to pretending to have a normal Thanksgiving dinner and eating the food my mother had spent all day preparing.

But those times were forgotten now. Blotted out. In 1999 I only felt my mother's sadness—and even my father's sadness—at losing me.

As such, I had a strong, repeated urge to step outside and call them and let them know that I loved them. The funny thing is, I didn't really even know *if* I loved them anymore. I wasn't really sure what I felt toward them. I only knew that at some level they had treated me disrespectfully too many times and that I wanted to be away from them. But it wasn't a great, clear feeling of assuredness I had. I felt lost in a black cloud of confusion and ambivalence and sadness of my own.

I talked a bit about my feelings with my friend, and that helped. He suggested to me that I just try to make it through the evening and not worry too much about the night or the future—just take it a couple hours at a time. And I could do that. And I did do that. But it was hell. It was a ruined holiday, in a way. Yet at the same time, it proved to be such a valuable holiday in the long run, because here I am, more than a dozen years later, remembering it as a bellwether for my future progress—and a template that encapsulated many valuable lessons. I made it through that holiday and through it I learned that I could survive my guilt without calling them, that I would not crumble under my pain and that I could, for at least a few hours at a time, make the choices I wanted for my life, even under extreme, embedded family pressure.

But why did I feel *so much* guilt? Why do so many people feel such guilt on the holidays? The psychology of inappropriate guilt is fascinating.

Here I think of Shawna, age 31, a biochemist whom I met through some mutual online friends.

"I was raised to deny my right to be my own person," she said. "I was not allowed to be my own independent entity who made decisions in my own best interest. They always told me I was special and could do anything in life with my talents, but what they never said was that I was always, forever, expected to stay close to them: to make them happy. *I was not allowed to break away from them.* That was a crime: the basic crime. And the punishment for that crime was that I would feel guilty. And they taught guilt to me by implanting a metaphorical psychological microchip in my psyche. Anytime I didn't do what they wanted they pressed the "guilt" button on that microchip, and I felt guilty. *Guilty as hell.* So later on, when I was breaking away from them, everything was so confusing for me. For a while I thought it was because I was female, like females were trained to feel guilty or something, but then when I got older and could see past my college feminism I realized they did an even worse number on my brother. He's so paralyzed by guilt and selflessness that he can't even take a single step away from them without shutting down emotionally and running back to them with his tail between his legs. And what's worse is that he has no clue of any of this. His emotional paralysis blinds him. He's totally hooked into their system."

"I'm curious about your brother," I said, "but I'm more curious how you resolved the guilt."

"Well, I stayed away from them and I studied myself," she replied. "I avoided them pretty intensely, and most especially on the holidays, because that's when I felt the worst. That and on their birthdays—and Mother's Day sucked also. Talk about guilt and loads of crappy other feelings. For the longest time, in the first years of my breaking away from them, all holidays were terrible for me. I felt like shit the whole day, and usually the day afterwards too, and I hate to admit it, but I used to get high on the holidays to blot out the pain. But then I started working through my feelings. It took me a while to convert that mental anguish into some kind of awareness of my actual unconscious psychological dynamics and to convert this awareness into conscious learning. But all that pain, the pain of guilt especially, was helpful, which I never would have imagined before. It seems so counterintuitive. But at some point I started to figure this out."

"And your brother?" I asked.

"He's a lost cause," said Shawna, shaking her head. "I hate to say it, but I had to give up on him—mostly, I realized, because he gave up on himself. My parents consider him the best little boy ever—and he's 36 now, an engineer like my dad—but he's lost and miserable. Yeah, he works a fancy job and has a wife they like and kids they go gaga over, but he's fucked up in his head. Totally unhappy just beneath the surface. In the same way most people are. I could actually see him committing suicide if his façade broke down—though he works hard to keep it all snugly in place."

"And how does he treat you?"

"It's complex. He loves me and he hates me. He loves me because we do share a lot of good memories from way back when—and also because somewhere, deep inside of himself, he respects me for what I'm doing. Or maybe this is only my fantasy that someday he's going to wake up and get healthier. Maybe that healthy side of him doesn't really even exist. Maybe I just wish it did. I do know, though, that I can speak much more confidently about the side of him that hates me. That's the sick side of him. In that side of him, the side of him that the world sees and that he's aware of and that defines him as a functioning person in the world and that his wife knows, well—he really does hate me. He's always hinting that I'm a lesbian, even though I'm not, as if somehow me being a lesbian would explain to him why I've ditched our family. He's also really cagey around me seeing his kids; he keeps me at arm's length from them, like I'll somehow pollute them—with that most dangerous thing: the truth. Yet at the same time he's critical as hell that I stay away from our parents. He sees everything through his weird lens of denial and rage. He's really a lot like my parents. They remade him in their image, and they reward him for it. He's one of those normal people who's destroying our planet—happily and obliviously. And he goes to all the holiday events and his wife and kids are right in the middle of all their celebrations, and me—well, I'm self-exiled."

"Does it make you angry?" I asked.

"Not so much anymore," replied Shawna, shaking her head. "But to be honest, sometimes, yes—when I'm not simply feeling relieved and happy to be away from them. But yes, sometimes things do make me angry, like when I hear that my parents are spending huge amounts of money on his kids, putting them in private school and buying them fancy vacations and stuff like that. And of course I get none of their money, not that I really even want it, though of course, sometimes, I admit it would be nice. But anyway, he'll probably inherit everything of theirs. I know my parents, and know that they'll punish me by cutting me out of the will. He'll get the house, the money—all that. And thinking about that kind of stuff can make me angry. But when my anger comes up I find it very valuable: it helps me dissolve my inappropriate guilt and return to a state of sanity. My anger points me in the right direction—and then I have to walk forward. Free and independent. And money can't buy that."

Chapter 20: What If Your Parents Are Growing?

Occasionally I meet parents who are delving into deeper inner work, not only exploring their childhoods and childhood traumas but also exploring the damages they have committed on their children. These parents pique my interest, because they provoke the following question: *Should we still break from our parents if they are on the same journey as we?*

The answer for me comes down to two new questions. The first and most important is this: *Do we feel like breaking from them?*

If we feel like breaking from them, then I believe that trumps all other questions—because we must honor our desire for independence. But if we are only ambivalent about breaking from them, and are considering some sort of relationship with them, the following question will inevitably have some relevance: *How serious are they about getting real?*

Here I think of Kevin, a divorced fifty-year-old father from Seattle who found me through my website a couple of years ago.

"What you share on your website is obvious," he initially wrote, "and deep down I've always known it but just couldn't admit it to myself. I committed a crime on my son by having him before I had healed my childhood wounds. This wasn't fair to him and I suffer with this knowledge. I've already admitted to him what I've done and I will do anything to make it up to him."

The problem I observed, though, when I later met Kevin and his son in person when I was passing through Seattle, was that he wasn't telling the full truth. He wasn't really willing to "do anything" to make it up to his son, and even had he been willing to "do anything" it would have been too late. The damage was already done, decades earlier. His son, age 25, had long since been crushed into normalcy: he was uninterested in delving into his past or grappling with the deeper realities of existence and instead focused on having a conventional career, dating, getting married and having children himself.

"Dad," I heard him say, "give it a rest! You were a fine father. You did the best you could and that's why I love you."

And although Kevin protested, I learned over time by watching and listening to him that secretly he felt comforted by this. Secretly he didn't really want his son to delve into the world of childhood pain, because Kevin liked keeping a comfortable relationship with him. He needed his son too much. His son made him feel safe and happy and stable, a sort of proof of his own validity as a person. His son was also, in a sense, his primary social world. His son was devoted to him and helped him keep the deeper pains of his own unresolved existence at bay. And although Kevin had eased some of his guilt by admitting a sketch of his crimes to his son, he had no intention of giving him the greatest parental gift: devoting his own life to getting honest to his core at whatever the cost.

Frankly I've never seen a parent do this. I think it might just be too difficult for them.

Meanwhile, Kevin's behavior is personally familiar to me. When I was 27, five years after my mother got sober in a twelve-step program, she did a "Ninth Step" with me, admitting her wrongs in order to make amends.[16] She created a list of the ways in which she'd harmed me and she read it to me. Some of the list items included her having been an out-of-control substance abuser, having been sexually inappropriate with me, having shown a poor example of a marriage partnership to me, having violated the boundaries of some of my childhood friendships and having repeatedly lied to me about all sorts of things. I remember several of my friends in Al-Anon, the self-help program for families of alcoholics, labeling me the luckiest guy in the world. Imagine, the unheard-of had happened: my mother not only got sober but actually fessed up!

But my luckiness was questionable. Instead I felt that her action was somehow sick. Yet at first I couldn't put my finger on exactly *why* it was sick. Instead her admission overwhelmed me, so much so that I dissociated: I split off from myself emotionally. All I knew was that I could hardly speak to her about what she was admitting and I certainly was not feeling joyous. This motivated me to study my own feelings and figure out why I felt sick when it seemed I should, according to my peers,

---

[16] Alcoholics Anonymous's Ninth Step: "Made direct amends to such people wherever possible, except when to do so would injure them or others." For more, see: Alcoholics Anonymous (1980). *The Big Book*. New York: Alcoholics Anonymous World Services, Inc.

feel grateful. I journaled about it, talked it over with healthier friends, listened to their input and meditated on it throughout my daily activities.

In hindsight, a year or two later, what I determined was this: her admission was actually a preemptive strike. I felt (and feel more strongly now, many years later) that she recognized better than I did that I was putting together the pieces of my past and getting savvy to her behavior and how it affected me. I was journaling like mad, analyzing my dreams, living on my own and paying my own way in life. I didn't feel I needed her so much anymore. I was starting to read Alice Miller and Judith Herman around this time and was, in general, reading several psychology and psychotherapy books a week. I was also just becoming a therapist and was interning at a clinic in New York City for traumatized Vietnam combat vets. I lived, worked and breathed trauma and I had just started connecting it all to my own life. My traumas may not have been as extreme as those of the vets I spoke with daily or as those in Judith Herman's *Trauma and Recovery*, but my traumas definitely fell on the trauma continuum; I knew that. It was undeniable. As the result of this I started standing up for myself more in relation to her and to others who had traumatized me. And mostly I stood up by pulling away: keeping myself away from them.

And my mother didn't like it. It made her feel uncomfortable and scared and caused her to become nasty toward me, which caused me to stand up for myself even more: with boundaries, more distance and, when necessary, rational, thought-out replies. This drove her to distraction, because her old pattern of crushing me in order to pull me back in was no longer working as easily as it once had. I believe that as the result of my obvious external transformations and my more subtle internal ones my mother sensed correctly that I would soon be confronting her in a more serious way.

And here is my analysis of what had gone through her head before she did her "Ninth Step" with me: she realized, largely unconsciously, that if she, of her own volition, admitted some measure of what she'd done to me then I would be rendered powerless to blame her for anything. How, after all, could you blame (that is, hold responsible) a seemingly honest, open, forthright, admitting mother who is taking a seemingly profound step at holding herself responsible? I couldn't consciously grasp this subtext at the time, but my unconscious did. And my emotions felt it—immediately. I felt I was being manipulated by opposing currents of psychological pressure and I hated her for it. But at the same time the wounded part of me that still wanted her to love me, and even believed I *needed* her to love me, went into a panic because hating her meant that I would lose her. This was the double bind she placed me in. For that reason I dissociated.

I am now convinced that my mother had no real intention of healing or changing; time has shown me that. It is more than a decade later and I have seen little evidence that she has emotionally grown. Meanwhile, a real, direct amends by her—that being the purpose of the "Ninth Step"— would have been to stop manipulating me and instead to devote herself fully to healing her own childhood wounds. But to me that seemed far from her mind. Instead, I observed her continuing with a variety of other unhealthy behaviors, including staying close to her own alcoholic parents and remaining just as dishonest as ever about the realities of her behavior, which, incidentally, has continued to be manipulative. Yes, she made those admissions to me, but they were only a psychologically decked-out Trojan horse meant to lure me back in and reinvade my mind.

"That is a very harsh assessment," many people have told me. People: people who are still emotionally wedded to their parents. People who have not broken away. People who cannot side with their hurt inner child. People who have sold themselves out to keep alive their relationships with their primary traumatizers in order to keep their traumas at bay and their denial-armor in place.

Here is where it helped me to have friends on my side who had enough emotional distance from their families of origin to be able to see in perspective what I was talking about.

"Right on," said one. "Given what you've told me and what I've observed about your family, your assessment is right on the money."

"Trust yourself and your feelings," said another. "Your mom sounds like bad news."

But what if a parent really *is* healing?

The truth is, I haven't yet seen it to any great degree. I have not seen a parent who has taken that quantum leap of doing so much inner work that he or she really is in a position to have a healthy, boundaried relationship with his or her children. Instead, in every case I've seen, the very fact that parents had children in the first place is the sign, as I've written about earlier in this book, that they were not and were unlikely ever to become fully committed to healing their wounds. They reproduced to take the easy way out, to get off the highway of life and to avoid dealing with their ancient pain. They had children to cement their sick normalcy—which they didn't even realize existed—into place. Their children became receptacles for their unresolved and largely unconscious feelings and dreams and fantasies from their own childhoods and their children, to some degree, and usually to a great degree, remain these receptacles to the end.

And the other problem with parents, especially parents of younger children, is that even if they *were* emotionally committed to healing their childhood wounds, they wouldn't have enough free energy or time to do it properly. After all, as every parent will say, quite realistically: it takes a huge amount of time and energy to raise a child. It alone is a full-time job.

Yet some parents *do* take their healing more seriously than others, as evidenced by the number of parents who read and love the writings of Alice Miller. (I myself know many such parents, some of whom have gone quite far on the healing paths.) Yet even this is something of a farce, as Alice Miller herself was quite a limited parent, as evidenced not just by her own son's public admission,[17] but because she herself consistently lets parents off the hook through her writings, sending them the incorrect message that it's okay to become a parent first and to heal later.[18] In this vein, my own mother had Alice Miller books around the house when I was a teenager in the 1980s, and what good did they do me? Although I cannot remember speaking about these books with her, I can only imagine that they gave her more fodder to focus on herself as a victim of her parents and to avoid focusing on herself as an abusive parent. And even if I am dead wrong here and Alice Miller did help my mother grow up and take some more adult responsibility, for my sake it was, at some primal level, too little, too late.

For parents to have a healthy relationship with their child they have not only to heal their childhood wounds first, but then to realize fully how they have replicated them on their own child and how they continue to replicate them. And then they have to fully change their behavior. I've never seen any parent do this. To make matters worse, I see massive disincentive for most parents to do this.

For instance, had Kevin, the father from Seattle, become deeply healthy his son would almost certainly have felt betrayed by him. Had his son's feelings of betrayal been converted into words, he might have said: "What

---

[17] See the interview with Martin Miller here: *Mein Vater, ja, diesbezüglich.* Der Spiegel. May 3, 2010. http://www.spiegel.de/spiegel/print/d-70327191.html

[18] For more on this subject, see my essay on Alice Miller: http://www.wildtruth.net/alicemiller

right do you have to raise me one way, train me on pain of rejection to build up a fake personality and then, when it suits you, suddenly reject the person I've become? Screw you! You should have gotten healthy before you had me!"

And what if my own mother had gotten real? What if, instead of growing more fake and manipulative in her so-called sobriety she had instead gotten fully honest with herself, broken from her own parents, devoted herself to her own healing and actually accomplished it? Would I have then accepted her back?

The answer I can best come up with is this: no and yes. The "no" part is simple: there is no "accepting her back" because for me there is no *going back*. That time is done, over and complete. My childhood is over and our parent-child relationship is over. It can never be rekindled, no matter how healthy she becomes. I have moved on.

But I see the "yes" part as follows: yes, because if I fully healed from the wounds she caused me and she fully healed from the wounds her parents caused her, I could conceivably accept her in my life as a newfound ally. But our relationship would no longer be one of mother and a son. It would instead be a relationship between two voluntary equals. It would be a friendship. And I could imagine myself liking this—assuming, of course, that just being around the person who had the most profound effect on traumatizing my childhood didn't trigger the hell out of me, which, to be honest, it might do for the rest of my life no matter how much healing I do.

But that said, could my mother heal fully? I imagine, given what I know about her, that this will not happen with any greater degree of likelihood than scientists bringing dinosaurs back to life. I spent enough years wishing for my mother to get real, fighting for it and bashing my head into the wall over it to try to push it to happen. Instead I woke up and broke away—and thankfully not too late.

Yet I know some adult children who claim to have this type of relationship with their parents.

"My parents and I now have a mature relationship," they say. "We hang out, we talk about everything and we're equals. We're friends now."

Although there might be some grains of truth in what they say, in the bigger picture the main thing I observe them expressing here is their denial, that is, the degree to which they failed to break away and become freestanding individuals who have much of a deep perspective on their inner worlds. From what I observe, in their psyches they still remain hurt little children who haven't faced the realities hidden in the depths of their being. Thus primarily I hear their dissociation speaking. When I hear details of their stories I gain confirmation that their parents have changed only minimally. And their denial of this reality goes to show that so too have they.

But this said, I still do hope that parents work to get real. It may not bring them back into closeness with their children, but it does serve the world. Anyone who gets real, who heals and breaks from the lies of their past and from the people who harmed them, serves the world in a positive way. And the world needs it.

Chapter 21: Will I Ever Go Back to My Parents?

I get asked this question all the time. And sometimes in my private moments I ask it to myself. I guess another way of phrasing it would be to ask myself if I feel my break from my parents is permanent. Or, perhaps another way would be: "What might motivate me to return to having some sort of relationship with my parents?"

In tackling this question, I want to share something that I've learned over the years: that I don't make vows. I have done a lot of things in the past fifteen years that few people do, and one thing I have learned during this time is that nothing is necessarily permanent. Even the most intense things. I stopped drinking alcohol and smoking cigarettes for more than ten years. And as I mentioned earlier, I became celibate. I also journaled every day. For years it felt like a weird day to me if I didn't journal—and didn't journal several thousands words at a time. And there was a two-year period in which I didn't masturbate. It was almost like I took a vow to live my life these ways; but I never did take a vow. Why lock myself in? I preferred to live according to how I felt, and how I felt was an unfolding, organic process. If something felt right, deep inside me, I tried it. If it continued to feel right I continued on the path. But if it felt right to try something I'd previously stopped, I tried it.[19] This has been valuable for me. It has helped me to learn and grow.

The same holds true in my relationship with my parents. Although I haven't seen them in more than four years, if I felt it right to return to them, if only for a visit, I would. And I have thought of some scenarios that could happen even today that might get me to return. Although I lack desire to see them now, if I heard that either of them were dying I would probably return. Perhaps I would want to say goodbye. After all, for many years of my life both of them were the two most important people, aside from myself, in my world. I could imagine myself not wanting to miss the opportunity to talk with them one last time, hear anything they had to say—and maybe exchange a few ideas.

My grandmother died a few years ago at the age of 96, and I am grateful that we had the chance to speak on the evening of her death. She was still conscious and coherent—and wanted to speak with me. We were able to talk for a half-hour. Frankly, it was amazing for me, on a lot of levels. I had not spoken with her in about a year at that point, because she was so strongly on my parents' side in my conflict with them that I found it toxic to interact with her. But when I considered that she was dying, and that she and I had had some very positive times together in our history—we

---

[19] I want to make clear, though, that sometimes when I ended a major pattern of behavior, such as not masturbating, I felt a lot of mixed feelings, such as confusion, guilt, even shame. Changing courses in life often hasn't been that easy for me. But sometimes, to be fair, it has felt okay, that is, lacking in much pain or ambivalence.

had been quite close at various points in my life—I wanted to have one last opportunity to connect with her.

In that last interaction she actually confronted me: she said that it was her dying wish that I return to my mother. I said I could not promise that. She begged me to promise it, but I couldn't do it—and wouldn't. It would not have been honest. I also told her that she had some responsibility, some big responsibility, for some of the things that had happened in my family history, and that rather than push me to forge a false bond with someone who was not healthy for me I felt she would do better to get real with herself about her own role in the family—even now, while she was dying. Perhaps, I suggested, she herself could talk with my mother—her daughter —honestly, about this. My grandmother refused, and instead begged me once more to return to my mother, which again I could not promise. It was extremely sad for me, horrifying even, but also fascinating. She knew she was leaving this life, she didn't believe in God or an afterlife, I felt she knew this was her final chance to bloom as an honest person, yet she was still as committed to bowing down to the troubled dynamics of my family as she ever had been. Getting more real was out of the question for her.

But perhaps some people feel I should have lied to my grandmother and just made her happy in her dying request. I disagree. In fact, I addressed this to her directly. "Betty," I said (as that is what I had called her since childhood), "I can't and won't lie to you and tell you something that is not true. Too much of our relationship has been based on honesty for me to lie to you now. I respect you, I respect myself, and I respect our relationship too much. So I'm going to tell you straight: I will not promise you that I will go back to my mother."

However, this was not how our conversation ended. Instead it ended with me telling her that I loved her and her telling me that she loved me. We were both crying. The truth is, as much as I detested her for her weakness and for the traumas she'd foisted on my family system and on me in particular, I still, in some part of myself, loved her. I loved the best in her. And I still cared about her. And I still empathized with her life situation—not just the fact that she was dying but that she was a trapped woman—trapped by her own childhood traumas, trapped by the limitations of her generation and all that that entailed for her gender, trapped by her fears and denial and trapped by the rotten things she'd done, most of it passively, to her own children and by extension to me. I felt for her. But frankly, very little short of her dying, at that point, would have brought me out of my familial isolation in order to connect with her.

As such, I believe—though I do not know, because sometimes it is hard to be sure of these deeply emotional and important things—that I would also reconnect with my parents if they were conscious and dying. In fact, I am almost sure of it. It would be too important for me to miss.

But would other things bring me close to them again? Right now I cannot imagine much. I guess I would consider reconnecting with them if they started devoting their lives to inner healing, but, as I mentioned earlier, this seems so farfetched as to be impossible. So I don't consider it. But if they did, well, then yes, I'd give them a chance—probably a wary chance, small, and if they handled themselves well I might let them back in a little more. Or then again, I might not, not even then. In some ways my life is so good now—so much happier, healthier, more relaxed, more boundaried, more gentle, more self-respecting, more healing-oriented, more joyous—that it just doesn't seem worth it. Almost like they lost their chance with me.

But I can consider an exception here: that sometimes I have a strong desire to get information from them. I want to ask them questions about my childhood. I want to know more about their history. I want to ask them more about their parents, their siblings, their thoughts, their successes and errors, their fears. I did a lot of this already in my twenties and into my thirties—and they also told me a huge amount about themselves and their history when I was a child—but still, I often have more questions. Now that I am in my forties I have different thoughts, different questions, new perspectives. Sometimes, as crazy as this might sound given my point of view and the subject matter of this book, I even want to ask my parents advice; I admit that at times it pains me that I cannot ask them. The reason I feel that I cannot is that it would be too much of a sacrifice for me. Going back simply isn't worth it. They're too toxic for me. Or more clearly put, having a relationship with them is too toxic for me. Could that change someday? I'm not sure. I doubt it. I know that for years whenever I consider reconnecting with them the answer comes back clearly: no. But if I come across as somewhat ambivalent in this chapter, it's probably because I am. This subject matter is not simple. My parents behaved as monsters with me in some ways, but some parts of them were genuinely good. And I cannot forget that. So again, I acknowledge the loss. It is a painful and profound one.

Nevertheless, in a way I think of myself as having divorced them. I considered titling this book *Divorcing Your Parents*, but that seemed a bit more harsh than the present title, and it also too strongly equated the breaking away process with romance. But there are some parallels. I know some people who have divorced spouses, sometimes in a very ugly, messy way, yet who, years later, have a more or less neutral or pleasant relationship with them. Sometimes they can even spend time together occasionally, maybe have a cup of tea and talk—about old times and even present times.

I sometimes wonder if I could ever have that kind of relationship with my parents. I'm not so sure. At least from my perspective on life now, I cannot imagine it. One way in which I think the divorce analogy breaks down in the context of this book is that a marriage is a far less intimate thing than a child-parent relationship. A marriage, even a very hurtful, disturbed one, entails a far less intense power differential than a child-parent relationship, and also, in almost all cases, begins infinitely more voluntarily than a child-parent relationship begins—from the perspective of the child, that is. After all, no child asks to be born; not one ever. And while we can also easily argue that child brides don't wish to marry middle-aged men, and thus their marriage is not voluntary, I consider that form of child abuse so extreme that to me it is not a real marriage but a form of slavery.

But is it possible that in ten years or twenty years, if I continue on my healing path and my parents heal some more—and are still alive—that I could spend some time with them? Yes, I can consider it. After all, I have taken no vows. Ultimately my guides for life are the feelings that arise from the heart of my true self. And I have lived long enough to know that sometimes those feelings, and the needs arising from those feelings, can change. So in that way I don't want to box myself in and speak with full confidence about my future—because I don't have it.

Chapter 22: Looking Forward

As I close this book, I want to reflect briefly on my process of writing it. Over the past eight weeks, which is the time I spent creating the bulk of it, I have felt two main things: excitement and terror. These intense and contradictory feelings have reminded me of how important and how taboo this subject matter is. Breaking with our parents is important because it lays the framework for an entire personal and social revolution by which to uplift ourselves as individuals and as a species, yet taboo because it directly contradicts the lies keeping ourselves and our entire species stuck.

Part of my personal terror arises because some of these lies still live within me. I am not just contradicting my parents and parents in general by writing these words: I am also contradicting the unhealed, dishonest, defended sides of myself. Although I am afraid, perhaps realistically so, that my parents will somehow try to destroy or discredit me for outing our family secrets, my deeper fear is that if they and the world reject me I will not be there to love myself. This reminds me of three things: (1) how much they wounded me, (2) how wounded I remain, and (3) how much healing I still have in front of me.

Thus, for the purposes of writing this book, my worst enemy has been the wounded sides of myself—that is, the troubled and traumatized sides of them (1) that are still embedded in my head, and (2) that I have yet to break away from. Had I not been so personally terrified of the taboos I was breaking I would have likely written this book twice as quickly and twice as fluidly. Instead I wrote it in spite of my fears, which made the work a lot harder. Although the writing has been a labor of love, because I so believe in the value of the topic, it really has been a labor. Many nights it brought me nightmares, many times while sitting in front of my computer I dissociated in the middle of a paragraph and many times I wondered if I would or actually could go ahead and publish it at all.

At the same time, my lack of full healing has, I believe and I hope, made this book better. When I write about the horrors of the family system, I write with immediacy, not just about distant others and "their" problems. I am writing about me: my own rich, honest, present-tense, personal life. When I write about how scary it is to cut off your parents I feel that fear because I have lived it and to some degree still live it.

Meanwhile, when I conceived of writing this book my intention was to provide others an ally. Little did I know I would be providing one for myself as well. This has been a gift for me, because I have needed it. Although I have some good friends who support me on my journey, they are such an extreme minority in this pro-family, pro-denial, adult-centered world that I often feel very alone. I often keep quiet in public just to be able to function—and to protect my hard-won ideas. I have learned the hard way that if I speak up too loudly about the truth of the family system —or the fact that I've been creating this book—I get attacked and end up depleting resources defending myself to people who aren't even interested in or available for rational discussion.

Our world really is very sick. Most people are so incredibly defended against facing the painful truths of their childhood that the social revolution of which I write can sound like the pipe dream of a fanatic. Yet is it a pipe dream? And am I a fanatic?

I answer "no" to both questions, for the following three reasons.

First, I have—to a large degree, perhaps larger than I even realize—truth on my side. The motives and behaviors of modern parents may be an unwelcome or unpleasant truth to many, but it's the truth. I've been studying this my whole adult life, hungrily looking to prove myself wrong, and I have not been able to. The reason I have been looking to prove myself wrong is that *if* I could find parents innocent, my own parents first and foremost, I would be able to live a much simpler, calmer, less terrifying, easier, gentler life. I'd get in a normal relationship, be a normal guy, have normal sex, have normal kids, make normal money, live in a normal home, have normal interests, have normal friends and be normal. There is a wonderful comfort in playing by the rules. Part of me has long wanted this, even longed for it. It's not fun to be an outlier, a borderline social outcast, a slightly camouflaged pariah. I never chose to be these things. Instead these things chose me, because I wasn't weak or sick enough to deny reality. The fact is, I'm pretty strong and pretty healthy. And writing this book has reminded me of that too.

Second, I am not fighting for a bizarre, fringe cause, which is what fanatics do. I am fighting for a cause that affects all of us everyday. In fact, this cause affects us more than any other, because it is *the* root social problem. This is the core of why our species is traumatized and has become so destructive. This is the core of our denial and the core of our mistreatment of our own selves, each other and our planet. Because I see this clearly, I fight for this cause because I really see no other hope for changing our world. If we as a species do not revolt against the insanity of our parents, heal our wounds and become sane, what logical hope is there for us?

Third, as regards whether or not my hope is based on a pipe dream, I see the possibility for human change *as very real*. And here is how I see it unfolding:

(1) The healthiest, strongest, most mature, most aware people devote themselves to breaking from their parents, healing from their wounds and becoming real. The people in this group are the icebreakers. They are lonely, isolated and often frightened, because they have so few allies. But they persevere through a combination of personal force, creativity and experimentation. They are good people, they are strong people and they are reasonable people. And they will stop at nothing.

(2) As these people become healthier, they become the vanguard representatives of a new species. They become the emotional leaders of our new path and they provide guidance, example, inspiration and alliance to struggling others.

(3) As more people break from their parents, the movement of new, mature, independent people grows. They begin to form communities based on previously unseen models of human relationships. Their values differ profoundly from the sick norm and they know it and they love it.

(4) Rather than have children, these people work to raise the unhealed child within themselves and to assist others in doing the same. They love children, as do all people who love their child within, but they focus *not* on making more children but instead on growing up.

(5) The movement spreads, because truth is stronger than lies and health is stronger than illness. More and more people follow their example and eventually the population of self-actualized, non-traumatized people reaches a tipping point in which the world's taboos reverse. Suddenly mild child abuse and mild neglect, as opposed to speaking out against them, become taboo. I suspect this tipping point would come when self-actualized people comprise about one-tenth of one percent of the world's population, that is, one out of every thousand people. The reason I pick such a low percentage is that anyone who has significantly healed his childhood traumas has about a thousand times more passion than someone who has not engaged in healing. Thus, in terms of relative power, a very small number of healthy people can dramatically overpower, outthink, outdebate, out-sing, out-create, out-write and out-love the far, far majority of normals.

(6) Having passed the tipping point, the human movement toward self-actualization now expands at an explosive level. The minority rapidly becomes the majority. Healing from childhood wounds is now a thousand times easier because the world now promotes instead of resists it. There is now social expectation to face our traumas, break from our parents, incriminate them for their damage to us, reconnect with our emotions and live the healthiest lives imaginable.

(7) Healthy people now become ready to have children — and they become model parents. My supposedly "high standards" for parenting become easily and naturally attainable. Children are raised without human-induced trauma. Cooperation becomes the norm, warfare ends, the rates of suicide and so-called "schizophrenia" evaporate into nothing, drug abuse becomes nonexistent, psychiatry and the mental health field shrivel as professions and kindness, empathy and love reign supreme.

Some call me fanciful; I call myself a visionary.